Problems,
God's Presence,
and Prayer

Problems, God's Presence, and Prayer

*Experience the Joy
of a Successful
Christian Life*

Michael Wells
Foreword by Sam Jones

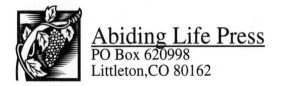

Abiding Life Press
PO Box 620998
Littleton, CO 80162

Published by Abiding Life Press
a division of Abiding Life Ministries International
P.O. Box 620998, Littleton, CO 80162

Sixth printing, February, 2004

Printed in the United States of America

Library of Congress Cataloging-in-Publication Data

Wells, Michael, 1952-
    Problems, God's presence, and prayer: experience the joy of a successful
    Christian life/Michael Wells; foreword by Sam Jones.

    p. cm.
    ISBN 0-9670843-1-8
    1. Christian life--1960- 2. Presence of God. I. Title.
    BV4501.2.W41818   1993
    248.4--dc20   93-31241

To the God of the weak

Contents

Foreword

When my friend Michael Wells sent me the manuscript of this book with a note asking if I would write the foreword, I had just finished reading his previous book, *Sidetracked in the Wilderness.*

Many Christians have been fooled by the idea that if they just don't think of the devil, he'll go away and won't bother them at all. I myself was a believer in this theory for a long time, until I realized that the devil is out to get Christians by hook or by crook. *Problems, God's Presence, and Prayer* is a book that can help those who have adopted such a false theory for their lives.

The message of this book rings loud and clear, and it is this: Take heed, Christian, the devil is after you; he wants to see you defeated and dethroned from the heavenly places in Christ Jesus in which you have been placed by the grace of God . . . and when that happens, you can't hide behind a theology of eternal security, but you may hide behind 1 John 1:9, "If we confess our sins, he is faithful and just and will forgive us our sins and purify us from all unrighteousness" (NIV). Mike Wells has taken this message around the world through his writings and personal visits.

Mike is a special person whose method of Christian communication is unique. It is a method that missiologists and theologians have advocated in their books and classrooms, a method missionaries in foreign lands have tried for years, but to which they could not bring themselves without reservation. It is a method that can revolutionize modern missions and bring them back to the original style of Jesus of Nazareth. It is called *friendship*.

What a wonderful and sacred tool it is for evangelism, and how Mike Wells has personified it through his life and ministry by cultivating simple and genuine friendships!

Mike has touched religious pundits, rebellious youth, alcoholics, and agnostics alike with a God-given ability to look to the potential beyond an antagonism toward Christianity and see the value of a soul that needs Christ. I have watched him put away the temptation to take a cheap shot and the petty ambition to become a big shot; he is a servant and a friend, not a patron. He has no hired manager to say, "H-e-e-e-r-e is Mike," before he speaks.

Worship of the cult of success in our time has deceived a lot of Christians. Many Christians are unaware of the intricacies of the work of the devil amongst them, perhaps because they imagine the devil works in bars and dirty back alleys but not in neat places such as churches and Christian organizations. How wrong we have been. And if we apply the world's standard of success to Jesus and His earthly ministry, He was a colossal failure and a total waste. Who would have thought that a shameful execution on a Roman cross, as friends and family watched helplessly, was a success? But God was at work right there initiating the final victory over the devil's scheme even when the world was mocking Him.

There are many voices urging for our attention with an appeal to write, or better yet, call, and have the credit card ready for a quick way to success. Even some Christian persuaders use this technique to reach their goal of success and a name for themselves. *Visibility* is the watchword. "Reaching the world for Christ" is the excuse, all in the name of Jesus, to whom visibility meant hanging on a cross.

What a breeding ground for the devil and his angels—yes, I said *angels*—to get Christians off track. *Problems, God's Presence, and Prayer* analyzes this paradox of success and shows what it means to be really successful. The book can help readers examine the innermost recesses of their own hearts with honesty, psychological insight, and scriptural authority.

During my ministry with the Billy Graham Evangelistic Association, I had the privilege of meeting many genuine servants of God around the world. Mike Wells is one of them. I met him in the early eighties during one of my visits to Denver for a special meeting, representing Billy Graham and the Amsterdam World Conferences. During an unplanned session with Mike, I was impressed by his insight into the Scriptures and his understanding of human nature and the devil's attempts to defeat Christians. Our love and respect for each other grew during these many years through mutual concerns, friends, and partnerships in the ministry.

Are you a defeated Christian under threat from the enemy and in need of help? Are you offended and angry because of a broken relationship? Do you want to be completely free from bondage that the enemy may have brought upon your life and to experience the joy of a successful Christian life? If this is what you desire, I commend you to read *Problems, God's Presence, and Prayer*.

Dr. V. Samuel Jones
Billy Graham Evangelistic Association

Introduction

Before I became a believer, I was not particularly surprised by the chaotic circumstances of my life. That seemed to be what life was about. Everyone around me was going through the same things. From Christian friends, however, I heard a hopeful message. They said the cause of my disturbances was very simple: "You do not know God; therefore, you are like a man who continually tries to swim upstream in a compassionless current." The solution was equally simple: "Invite Christ into your heart and have life that is abundant, free from worry, fear, and even calamities." Those who witnessed to me of the love of Jesus and His saving power made it quite clear that I would be taken out of the life of emptiness and struggle that I was experiencing.

That was many years ago, and to be perfectly honest, my life has greatly improved since I became a Christian. However, it has not been and presently is not free from turmoil, defeat, times of loneliness, or even tragedy. In short, I still experience distress. I have learned, too, that this condition is not uniquely mine. I often disciple believers who are in the midst of family chaos, who are bound by sins they thought were put off long ago, who are under tremendous financial pressure, who are contemplating divorce, or who feel that God is nowhere to be found. Their lives are, according to them, anything but abundant.

What is the reason for believers' being in such a predicament? What case can be made in their favor? None of this is supposed to happen to those who want with all their hearts to follow God; is it? We have accepted Jesus as our very life; how can this be? Is there any good that could come out of such difficulties? Is there any way to reasonably explain our roller-coaster rides in and out of agitation? Could it be that the hand of God is somehow behind all we experience that is disturbing and perplexing? If only we could be assured that God is involved in our disappointments as part of His plan and that we are not merely controlled by the world environment—maybe then we could be encouraged in the midst of our problems.

The promise is that we *can* all be heartened, that there is a heavenly purpose for all our problems! Upon seeing the wonder, the wisdom, and the simplicity of it, we will rejoice that God has blessed us with problems. There is a divine ending planned for every difficulty. When this is realized, we can learn to appreciate times when hopes are dashed and frustrations run high.

Part 1

Problems
with a Purpose

1

Are Problems Normal?

What is the *normal* Christian life? Is it one that includes struggles, problems, and events that seem to assail the joy that we are told will be found in Christ?

Is it normal to have problems springing from such natural desires as food or sexuality, or to contend with uncontrolled thoughts or lack of discipline? Is it typical to be overwhelmed by emotional turmoil, hurts from the past, remembered failures, feelings of inferiority and insecurity, and even the fear of being rejected by God? Is it not unusual to struggle with finances, health, the annoying roommate, mate, or parent? These are all vexing questions for two essential reasons. First of all, we were usually wrestling with such things before we came to Christ, and who could have imagined such a struggle once we were in Him? Second, many authors, lecturers, and Christian leaders have implied that this type of experience is not part of the normal Christian life, but, rather, reveals the deficiencies of substandard faith.

While we are trying to understand the inadequacies of our
lives, we may hear the testimonies of victorious believers who
rarely mention any distressing experiences coming after conversion. The lives of these believers seem generally to have been
lives of victory, praise, and overcoming power! Therefore, many
of us, with the passing of time, come to accept the fact that we
are very abnormal believers: weak, not standing where we
ought, and lacking the ability, intellect, and discipline to live
the victorious life that would free us from problems. Then we
either give up or begin to look for the method that will enable
us to live a life of complete victory as defined by the experiences of certain brethren.

Those with problems, however, must take heart, for what
I have found throughout my walk with the Lord and interac-
tion with His people is, remarkably, that problems are a natural element of the believer's life. The normal Christian life is
not without struggle, is not free from failure, nor is it a life of
constant emotional highs. On the contrary, this life is filled
with adversity, but adversity with a purpose.

See what the apostle Paul says in 1 Corinthians 4:9–13:

> For, I think, God has exhibited us apostles last of all, as men
> condemned to death; because we have become a spectacle to
> the world, both to angels and to men. We are fools for Christ's
> sake . . . we are weak . . . [and] we are without honor. To this
> present hour we are both hungry and thirsty, and are poorly
> clothed, and are roughly treated, and are homeless; and we
> toil, working with our own hands; when we are reviled, we
> bless; when we are persecuted, we endure; when we are slan-
> dered, we try to conciliate; we have become as the scum of the
> world, the dregs of all things, even until now.

This is not a popular passage with the prosperity crowd,
but Paul reiterates his point when writing the Corinthians once
again: "We are afflicted in every way, but not crushed; perplexed, but not despairing; persecuted, but not forsaken; struck

down, but not destroyed; always carrying about in the body the dying of Jesus . . ." (2 Cor. 4:8–10).

What, then, is the normal Christian life? It will often be a life full of trouble. Once we understand that adverse events, people, health, and circumstances have a purpose in our lives, we can submit to the hand of God in them. Problems are normal!

Many times discomfort in the lives of Christians comes not so much from the problems as it does from their continual self-examination. They wonder what is wrong with them that God would allow such things to happen. Scripture is replete with inferences that we will suffer; today, however, this aspect of the average Christian life is often overlooked, preventing many from replacing their discouragement with encouragement.

Let me illustrate. When my wife and I were expecting our first child, we enrolled in a course on childbearing, which presented what my wife and I would experience during the birthing process, terminology the doctor would use, and how my wife could more effectively deal with the pain through a series of breathing exercises. The hospital was full of patients the night of our baby's birth, so we had only a cloth divider between us and a young woman next to us. As we went through the experience, my wife practiced the breathing techniques, and we both listened attentively to every word of the nurse and doctor. She will testify that all the preparation did not rid her of the pain, but it did have a calming effect on us by familiarizing us with what would likely occur. However, the young woman next to us screamed throughout her entire ordeal, for no one had told her what to expect. What we considered normal she believed was doing her harm.

Any growing believer is continually giving birth to a deeper spiritual life. Those who understand the place of pain will rest, knowing that the outcome will be something glorious. Those who are uninformed about the need for problems in life to perfect them will often go through life screaming, wondering what is happening, and complaining about the person or persons who got them into such a condition. Lacking in them is any joyful expectation of what will come after the pain is long gone.

Much is said in Christian circles about fruit-bearing. Many sincerely desire to bear fruit, showing themselves to belong to their Father in heaven. There is one aspect of fruit-bearing, however, that is often overlooked: It can cause much discomfort, even pain.

I have an apple tree in my backyard. The weather in our area this past year was exceptionally favorable for fruit trees. My tree became so laden with fruit that it was actually pulled a full eight inches out of the ground. If I had not tended to the branches that were near breaking, the tree would have been severely damaged. The apple tree suffered in order to bear fruit useful to others. It nearly died to give life. Spiritual fruit is not for our benefit but for the benefit of those around us. Like the tree, the more fruit we bear, the more the Lord may have us in a state of stress.

Pain is normal for the fruit-bearing believer, and so is a period of winter, which comes shortly after the fruit-bearing season. During winter it looks as though the tree has no life at all. Its animating force is hidden from sight in the deepest part of the tree's being—its roots. There it will remain for months, being strengthened for what will be revealed in the coming spring.

So few believers have learned to enjoy the winter, when there are no feelings, no fruit, no great expressions of life, but rather the silent and hidden work of God in the deepest part of man's being, his spirit! Winter is normal. Times of pain are normal. Dryness is normal. Adversity is normal. All are needed to release the life that the believer has hidden within—Christ's life.

As we submit to the normal Christian life and see in the midst of problems God's hand training, directing, and releasing Christ's life, we learn some of the deepest secrets possible. Much of what we could never understand by reading about the lives of great believers such as Paul will become real through our own experience.

I personally could never understand Paul's statement, "being reviled we bless." It was something that I had memorized, so my mind possessed it, but the truth had never made the journey eighteen inches from my mind to my heart until one day when a problem occurred. I was working in another country when I received a call from my wife informing me that a sum of money a friend was to pay me would not be handed over—ever! He was refusing to give to me what was mine. I had begun my journey with the confidence that while I was far away, my wife would be able to make the house payment, buy groceries, and meet other necessary expenses. This confidence was anchored in the ability of my friend to give me what was owed. On hearing the troubling report that I was not to be paid, my first response was fury. How could he? How dare he? Who did he think he was?

After concluding the conversation with my wife, I knew, because of my concern for home and my anger, I could not leave my room to go minister to the assembly of waiting believers. I fell to my knees and began to pray, telling the Lord of all my frustration. His peace slowly began to descend. In His light I could see light: Daily provision did not depend on man but on Him. God was my provider. What a glorious thought! I need not trust man, who is unreliable. I could trust God, who is always faithful. In that moment I was free from clamoring for the wealth of this world; the Son had set me free indeed. My response to the Lord was to decide that I would release the man from the debt when I returned home. I would, in essence, give him the money owed to me; that's how free I was from this man.

I got up with my heart—as Hudson Taylor once said—as light as my pocket, now ready to share with the believers my God, the God of all provision. When I entered the hall, a brother walked up to me and placed in my hand a check for the ministry that was ten times what I had lost. Talk about an

exchange rate! I was witnessing one of the most basic laws of
the kingdom at work: "For momentary, light affliction is producing for us an eternal weight of glory far beyond all comparison" (2 Cor. 4:17). That is, I was seeing the great imbal-
ance in the exchange rate of the kingdom of God, which is
always absolute. In giving little we receive much. If so much
could come out of this simple act of self-denial, what would
happen if I decided to take up the cross and deny self in all
areas pertaining to my relationships with others?

As I lay in bed that night, my heart was filled with grati-
tude for what earlier had been a problem. I asked the Lord to
bless this brother who had cheated me, for through his hand
had come such a great blessing. Without his actions I might
never have learned so fully that God is my provider, a lesson
that since that time has given me peace in the midst of many
adversities. As the words came out of my mouth to bless this
brother, I realized that Christ in me had accomplished Paul's
words, "when reviled we bless." Now I was more excited than
ever. When a problem comes, God will always work something
wonderful in me; therefore, I can bless those who curse me.

One day at the conclusion of discipling a woman who was
experiencing some marital difficulties, I gave her an assign-
ment. It was a seemingly small, simple thing to do. For the
coming week she was to kiss her husband each time he said
something negative or cutting to or about her. She percep-
tively joked, "Can't I have a book to read instead?" She knew
quite well the difficulties involved in doing the very smallest
of deeds requiring self-denial. Two weeks later she returned
and began to recount the changes that had taken place and the
new sense of freedom that she was beginning to experience
from the pressure to perform for others, from the feelings of
inferiority, and also from the anxiety that comes from pro-
tecting and propping up self. We could easily observe that the
fruit yielded from this problem with her husband far out-
weighed the misery that the problem had caused.

The normal Christian life is one of problems, but always remember that every problem has passed through the hand of a loving Father and carries with it, before it ever arrives, an express, intrinsic purpose. Those in the midst of affliction usually find the purpose hidden, but the experienced sufferer knows it will prove to be glorious. Problems are God's main tool for bringing us to the end of our own resources and into the deep experience of all His riches.

One of the most effective methods of horse-breaking is to put the wild horse in a chute, mount it, and release it into a sand-filled arena. It is interesting to watch the horse as it runs in circles, fighting the depths of the sand until lathered in white, and then finally, when it can no longer put one foot in front of the other, gives up. At this point the horse is no longer self-directed, but will allow the rider to dictate its every move.

So it is with brokenness in believers' lives. We come to Christ so full of self-effort, self-will, and energy. We are not ready to give the reins to the Holy Spirit. We must be put into situations that are very like the deep sand (troubles, circumstances, dealing with people), wherein every attempt to free ourselves brings only deeper exhaustion of the soul. In the end we are broken, each one willing to say, "I can't," and ready for the Holy Spirit to direct every move.

It will be at this point that soul (mind, will, and emotions), body, and the world are separated from the spirit. God has placed His very life in our spirits to make them treasure chests of what we as humans need and desire: love, security, acceptance, peace, and rest. Yet we are too accustomed to looking to ourselves and others, trying to discover these riches. So God allows everything outside the spirit realm to fail us, thus separating spirit from everything else and causing us to look only there for the meeting of our deepest needs. It is a painful process as we fail, but the result will be men or women in Christ who cannot be moved to activity outside the spirit. These believers can live above, not of, the things of the world, no longer milking their needs out of others, but filled to overflowing and able to give out of the abundance of their treasure-chest spirits.

This breaking process has been called the "dark night of the soul"; we walk in darkness with neither awareness of the Lord's presence nor satisfaction in all that exists outside the spirit. Here we come face to face with the fact that though our mouths proclaim peace in Christ alone, our hearts have clamored for the "lust of the flesh, the lust of the eyes, and the boastful pride of life" (1 John 2:16) to make us content. Comfort, rather than maturity and wholeness in God, has been the goal of life, which is why we accept the positives of life and despise all negatives. The breaking process will eventually cause us to look beyond the comfort zone and find that all we need in life is to know that God is on His throne.

Not long ago a friend told me that he had once lost several million dollars. The economy had taken a downturn in his part of the country, and he began to lose one business after another. He had not been alone in this predicament, for several of his friends had experienced the very same thing. He decided to meet with a friend who was in a similar situation and ask how he planned to salvage his fortune. The friend said that he owed a bank several million dollars and was going immediately to the bank to declare bankruptcy. He said that he would not try to hold onto anything but would tell the bank he was quitting his business. My friend was a bit befuddled by such a response and asked if it would not be better to put up a fight, plot, and work to hang on to his financial empire. The man explained his reasoning thus: "I owe the bank millions. I can work to pay it back and take on all the responsibility myself or declare bankruptcy. If I declare bankruptcy, the bank has too much invested in me to let me go down the tubes and will have the obligation, responsibility, desire, and vested interest to try to keep me from going completely under!" Within a few years my friend, though he fought to save his fortune, had lost it, but the man who had declared bankruptcy was a billionaire, thanks to the help from the bank.

I was walking in the mountains the next day, thinking of the conversation; it made sense that the bank, having invested so much, did in fact have a good reason for keeping the millionaire from going under. My next thought was *How much has God invested in us? He has invested His very own Son, worth so much more than millions of dollars. Having invested His Son, He has invested too much in each of us to allow us to go down the tubes.*

If we will only declare our own personal bankruptcy, stop working and plotting, and look to Him, He will complete what has been started. The very fact that God has invested His Son in us should silence every questioning thought that our minds might have. Will He help in my family? Will He help me financially? Will Christ grow in me? Will I ever be free from my sin and failure? Will I ever feel God is near? Of course God will see us through; He has too much invested in each one of us not to. "He who did not spare His own Son, but delivered Him up for us all, how will He not also with Him freely give us all things?" (Rom. 8:32).

2

Believers
Need Problems

Problems with a Purpose

David so wisely revealed, "In my distress I called upon the LORD . . . " (Ps. 18:6). Problems bring us near to God. They are calculated to bring us into the very presence of God. Once there, the burdened believer understands that there is nothing that God's presence does not cure. This is God's ultimate purpose for every problem.

When a person boards a plane to travel from a distant city back home, he feels relief and eager expectation, for the plane represents the means by which he will soon be with those he loves. Problems are analogous to the plane in that they are the means by which the believer can be transported into the very presence of God in heaven. Finding that His presence refreshes and restores, the believer will begin to give thanks for every situation, event, person, and calamity that propels him so near to God.

27

Some will disagree with the idea that God is involved in our problems, saying that people or events cause distress; they might even take the blame for some problems themselves, thus eliminating God's part in their suffering. They will conclude that it is up to them to fix whatever is amiss. This deception leaves believers struggling in their own strength with various situations, far from the overcoming power that God measures out so freely to those in His presence. Many believers spend their whole lives scheming to overcome problems in their own strength. They work hard to improve their conditions, and though they can never be completely successful, they relieve just enough of the pressure to avoid being prompted into the presence of God, where they would find abundant life.

Once we conclude that problems are tailor-made for the purpose of drawing us into God's presence, we will have an answer to 90 percent of the questions concerning distress. When I disciple someone who discloses to me a sin or short-coming that is conquering him, such as a horrific marriage, struggles at work, divisions in his church, or various mistakes he has made, one question immediately comes into my mind: *Father, how is this problem to bring this child of Yours closer to You?* What a wonderful secret to possess, knowing both the beginning (the problem) and what is to be the end (His presence). I need only construct for the discouraged believer a highway that will connect the two.

A believer with problems is blessed of God. Yes, truly blessed! If he has no place left to turn, has given up on himself and others, and has found out that the problems simply cannot be resolved in any earthly way, he can quickly be led to see there is only one hope for him—the presence of God. God is actually using the problems to drive the believer into His presence. What a blessed person! He need not look for God, for God has found him and will have him.

Imagine, if you will, a gardener who in the fall puts his most valued plants in a greenhouse, where they will be protected from the harsh winter. There they receive his constant care and continue to bear fruit, protected from a deadly environment. What if a plant could leave the greenhouse by its own free will? Winter would quickly bring about its death. So it is with believers. When in God's presence, we live within a spiritual greenhouse in a world that is pitted against God. Safe inside, we have God's comfort, protection, and fellowship, which allow for fruit-bearing. If we leave His presence, we will immediately experience the harsh realities of the world, of sin, of Satan, and of the flesh.

Too often we have made the mistake of trying to find an answer to the distress instead of returning to the presence of the loving Father, where no answer is needed. As Christians we should know the purpose of pain and the very reason for life, which is fellowship with God.

What a God we have! How privileged we are to have the God of all the universe focus His attention on us and pursue us to bless us! Sadly, it is true that God must engage in this pursuit, since many believers go through life avoiding Him. With their minds they want to give God His proper place, but at the same time they are drawn by their emotions to other people or plans to meet their deepest needs, thereby setting their own course for success and fulfillment apart from God. Man seems to love to meditate on this or that plan for inducing contentment, and he would devote his whole being to such scheming if not for one thing: problems. Like pain, they make man stop living for the future or dwelling on the past and take notice of the present. Problems make men choose God *now*.

Imagine being in a room with four walls and four doors. Three of the four doors are locked; the unlocked door is one through which you do not wish to go. You struggle, trying to open the other three until, out of frustration and often anger, you realize that you must choose the one door that is unlocked. On opening it, you discover to your surprise that this is actually the door that leads to the freedom you were so confident lay behind the other three. God uses problems to destroy our plans—which would never bring abundant life—and move us through the doorway that leads to His presence and true life. The prodigal son created his own distress, but it caused the glorious result of renewed fellowship with the father.

God is love! He wants us near so He can show us His love. Carnal man, however, is ignorantly self-sufficient. Problems make man realize that he is not an independent creature and that he needs the Creator to provide for him. Man cannot solve his own problems, let alone problems on a global scale. Problems allow us to see that we need God. If there were no problems that man could not overcome, surely man would never look beyond himself.

There should be no doubt that problems and distress are God's stronghold in the believer's life to drive him from self-sufficiency to the all-sufficient Father in heaven. "In my distress I called upon the LORD" (2 Sam. 22:7). "But in their distress they turned to the LORD God of Israel" (2 Chron. 15:4). "We will . . . cry to thee in our distress" (2 Chron. 20:9). "O LORD, they sought Thee in distress" (Isa. 26:16). "I called out of my distress to the LORD" (Jonah 2:2). Over and over we see the distress cycle taking place in Israel's history. The Book of Judges testifies to this cycle, for when things were going well, the people would soon forget God. Then they would cry out, God would deliver, and some time after the deliverance they would again forsake God. Problems are not intended to destroy us but to bring us near to God to be made complete.

There is nothing the presence of God does not remedy. Nothing! When we hear the commands of God, we can find ourselves overwhelmed and even running from Him, especially when past attempts to keep the commands yielded little or no success. We can begin to avoid God, not wanting to hear the words we fear: "You have failed." Herein lies a deep deception; we are not to improve our behavior before we come into God's presence, for that is impossible. Rather, it is God's presence that will improve our behavior.

Don't get cleaned up to draw near to God; draw near expecting Him to do the cleaning. When you are near the Lord, commands become promises. Instead of hearing, "You shall not commit adultery," and fearing that you might do so and be condemned, it is heard as a promise: "In My presence with My life and power, you will never commit adultery." See the difference? His presence gives confidence and hope.

The Scriptures are filled with men and women who, upon drawing near to God through problems and distress, found all that they needed for abundant life. The Israelites grumbled against the Lord in the wilderness. God heard their grumbling and prepared to act on their behalf; on the condition that they first draw near to Him. "Come near before the LORD, for He has heard your grumblings" (Exod. 16:9). "At twilight you shall eat meat, and in the morning you shall be filled with bread; and you shall know that I am the LORD your God" (Exod. 16:12).

Allow your problems to drive you to call upon the Lord, who will give relief and all that you need. "For what great nation is there that has a god so near to it as is the LORD our God whenever we call on Him?" (Deut. 4:7). Draw near to God, and the awareness of living in His presence will be so sweet, so beautiful, and so refreshing that problems will no longer be a concern. You will want to praise Him for distress, which in the past was viewed as a monster that would destroy but now is seen as the positive agent that brought about the nearness of God.

Problems Make Us Receivers

Is there a way out of our problems? What is it? Can we walk the path in our feeble condition? Will He accept us when we arrive? Yes! And the way is unbelievably simple. The answer is found in Him and not in ourselves. We are to focus on Him and not on our failures, frustrations, depression, or anx-

iety. In Him we will find the simple answer to overcoming
every obstacle.

Yes, His answer is simple, for in this moment His word to
you is, "Return to Me . . . that I may return to you" (Zech.
1:3). When you find yourself surrounded by problems, simply
say, "Lord, I return to you." That is all you need do to be assured that He will return to you. The word *return* in Scripture is a very simple little word meaning "to seek or call on."
A good illustration of the word would be my picking up the
telephone and giving you a call. By so doing I would return
to you, and if you answered the telephone, then you would
have returned to me. To return to the Lord is as simple as picking up the phone and calling Him. How much effort does it
take to pick up a phone, dial the numbers, and wait for the answer? It is within the grasp of most people.

God is not a God of the one-time remedy, but rather He
gives all that is needed in any one moment. We must call on
and return to Him moment by moment, staying in constant
fellowship to receive His constant help.

We can look at Scriptures that mention specific areas of defeat. God's prescription in each of the passages listed below is
the same—return. Then He will bring about the result. As you
look at the list, you may find items in the "Problem" column
that apply to you. I trust you will see that the solution to all of
these is to return to the Lord to receive the promised resolution. There is the deception that we can obtain those things
listed as "Result" through some plan or method of our own,
but it simply is not so. If it were a possibility, then God would
lose His strong hold on us, and we would soon go our own
way. We must see that the desired result of every problem is
the nearness of God, and when this nearness is achieved, at
that point and in His own time God is free to take away the
problem. God seeks the nearness of all men, not just a select
few. However, it is only a few who submit to God's purpose
of being brought near through their problems.

Scripture	Problem	Result
Deuteronomy 4:30–31	Distress	Compassion
Deuteronomy 30:4–6	Cursed	Restored, freed
1 Samuel 6:4	Sickness	Health
1 Samuel 7:3	Oppression	Deliverance
1 Kings 9:48–50	Sin	Forgiveness
2 Chronicles 6:24–38	Lack of commit-ment	Total commit-ment
2 Chronicles 30:6–9	Worry	Compassion for family and children
Job 22:23	Being lost	Being restored
	Unrighteousness	Righteousness
Psalm 6:3–4	Dismayed	Rescued
Isaiah 19:22	Not heard	God responds
Isaiah 44:22	Transgression	Cleansing
	Idolatry	Redemption
Isaiah 55:7	Wickedness	Pardon
Jeremiah 3:12	Failure	Grace replaces anger
Jeremiah 3:22	Faithless	Faithful
Jeremiah 15:19	Broken fellowship	Fellowship restored
Jeremiah 24:7	Half-hearted	Whole-hearted
Hosea 6:1	Wounded	Healed
Hosea 14:1	Stumbling	Free from sin
Malachi 4:6	Broken families	Hearts restored

Problems Prepare Us for God's Service

The Book of Judges records a most remarkable story. Samson, on his way to Timnah, was surprised by a young lion that came roaring toward him, but "the Spirit of the LORD came upon him mightily, so that he tore him as one tears a kid though he had nothing in his hand" (14:6). Samson was surprised by the lion, but perhaps equally surprised at what happened when the Spirit of the Lord came over him. Some time later when he returned that way, "a swarm of bees and honey were in the body of the lion" (v. 8). Samson ate until he was full, and upon finding his mother and father, he also fed them. Samson was sufficiently impressed by this whole adventure to compose a riddle about it. "Out of the eater came something to eat, and out of the strong came something sweet" (v. 14). The beast that was to destroy him became a source of nourishment for him and his parents.

We are told in 1 Peter 5:8, "Your adversary, the devil, prowls about like a roaring lion, seeking someone to devour." The devil, like Samson's lion, can seem to come from nowhere in the form of a problem, a temptation or sin, a circumstance, or even a person, with one purpose: to devour. However, if we stand fast in the midst of what would appear to be an overwhelming attack, the Spirit of the Lord will deliver us. "And after you have suffered for a little while, the God of all grace, who called you to His eternal glory in Christ, will Himself perfect, confirm, strengthen and establish you" (1 Peter 5:10).

After we have overcome, we may not be able to discern the reason for the problem for weeks, months, or perhaps ever while on earth. But the not knowing can itself further us along as we "grow up in all aspects into Him, who is the head, even Christ" (Eph. 4:15).

While visiting India, I asked one of my mentors a theological question. His immediate response was, "Before we answer the question, we must first discern if there will be anything of value obtained through the understanding the answer will bring!" After reflecting, I replied that the answer would have no direct impact on my life or the lives of others. The brother said, "Then these things are not to be known." I was amazed at how comfortable he was with not having an answer!

There are many things we question and try to understand that are not meant to be known. The answer, if received, would benefit us very little. For example, we might ask why a loved one died. Even if God were to give us a direct answer, it would not lessen our grieving, for only He can accomplish that. As we mature, we will be content with many unanswered questions.

In God's own perfect timing we will find that the problems we first thought would destroy us have actually empowered us and have even become a source of strength for others. We can then say with Samson, "Out of the eater came something to eat, and out of the strong came something sweet." Without the training that comes through living with problems, it is impossible for God's people to be fountains of life for others. We must struggle with challenges if we wish to minister to others. "Blessed be the God and Father of our Lord Jesus Christ, the Father of mercies and God of all comfort; who comforts us in all our affliction so that we may be able to comfort those who are in any affliction with the comfort with which we ourselves are comforted by God" (2 Cor. 1:3–4).

After reading Paul's writings and examining his life, we can say with confidence that great teaching comes through great weakness and suffering. Powerful teaching may have developed in the head, but it had to mature in the heart. This process rarely occurs except through difficulties.

In the mountains we have a mushroom called a puffball. It is full of life, but the life within is not released until the mushroom is completely dried out and crushed by the hoof of an elk or by a falling branch. Then the next rain can bring new fungal life to cover the forest floor.

So it is with us. The experiences of periodic crushing will release the power of the life that we hold within to break out in life around us. "For we who live are constantly being delivered over to death for Jesus' sake, that the life of Jesus also may be manifested in our body" (2 Cor. 4:11).

At the time the New Testament was written, smelters would heat up gold in order to extract the dross. After cooling, the gold would again be heated and more dross removed. This process continued until the smelter could see his reflection in the gold, at which time he would be assured that it was pure. The gold was not added during each heating, for it always existed in the ore. Rather, it was being more fully revealed.

Just so, the believer, at any given moment, possesses all of Christ that he ever will. However, the self-life hinders the expression of the great prize housed within every believer. God must remove all that is not of Him through periodic heating (problems). When the refining is over, more of Christ is revealed in the believer. The process is repeated over and over again.

The believer who has given up trying to solve his own problems allows them to draw him near to God for their resolution. He becomes a precious child to God. "In this you greatly rejoice, even though now for a little while, if necessary, you have been distressed by various trials, that the proof of your faith, being more precious than gold which is perishable, even though tested by fire, may be found to result in praise and glory and honor at the revelation of Jesus Christ" (1 Peter 1:6–7). This believer will experience Jesus' promise, "Truly, truly, I say to you, he who believes in Me, the works that I do shall he do also; and greater works than these shall he do; because I go to the Father" (John 14:12). For such a one, the self-life has been replaced by Christ's life, and he shares in the work of Christ on earth. It must be made clear to all who would enjoy such a life that the process of becoming spiritually productive includes problems.

Before we are given problems and then convicted of our own weakness in overcoming them, we rarely can see any of our own faults. We are self-righteous. But once we are convinced of our own shortcomings, we will associate with sinners, have compassion on them, and grieve over their sin. It is not enough that we hate sin with God's hatred (as many teach); we must also love sinners with the love of God's Son. Problems will bring us to a place of fruitful ministry in that love.

Problems Build Our Faith

Many believers deplore their lack of faith for the work to which God has called them. They want more faith in order to be more productive. Often, distressful circumstances are the very things God uses to build their faith.

All things that are received from God must be received by faith. In spite of the way things appear, we must trust that they will be ours. The Scriptures are full of promises to the child of God, but often when we try to grasp a promise and hold it as our own, a problem occurs that appears to negate the fulfillment of the promise. What is happening is quite simple: God is building our faith. If every promise were immediately realized, would we grow in faith?

Imagine placing a candy bar at the foot of a child's bed and telling him that tomorrow you will give him the candy to eat. Does your promise to provide the promised candy the next day call for the child to have faith? Certainly not, for the child can already see the candy.

God gives a promise, but we cannot immediately see its actuality, for "faith is the assurance of things hoped for, the conviction of things not seen" (Heb. 11:1). He then allows a problem that would appear to reverse His promise, but if we stand fast in belief, our faith will be built. Thus we often find that we will experience the reversal of a promise before we receive the fulfillment. It is this process that builds faith into us as God's people and, in the end, makes our lives truly abundant.

Recorded in Scripture are some examples of this principle at work in the lives of God's people. Reflecting on them will help us more easily understand the concept. Abraham suffered many reversals but stood fast in the promises of God until receiving their fulfillment. He believed that God would give him the land, and believing this small thing became the seed from which his faith in an infinite God would grow large. This is one message that Abraham brings all believers: If we trust God

in one small thing, that one small thing will be the beginning
of great and magnificent blessings. What happened, though,
after he received the promise of the land? He had to leave it
because of a famine, he gave his nephew first choice of the land,
and he had to go fight a war. Ultimately we find him asking,
"O Sovereign LORD, how can I know that I will gain possession of it?" (Gen. 15:8 NIV).

Joseph was promised in a dream that his parents and brothers would bow down to him, but much suffering, rejection
(including total spurning from the very brothers he had
dreamed were honoring him), and humiliation came between
the promise and its fulfillment.

Albeit with trepidation, Moses believed that God was sending him to deliver the Israelites from Egypt, but before he saw
the mission accomplished, the signs and wonders he'd been
given from the Lord had been matched by Pharaoh's magi-
cians, and the Israelites opposed him for making them odious
in Pharaoh's sight.

After Samuel anointed David because the Lord had chosen him to be king, did David rise up and sit on the throne?
No. Before he became ruler he was threatened with death over
and over by Saul. As he hid, his far-from-regal dwellings were
caves, and he became closely acquainted with hardships and
obstacles of many kinds.

The Holy Spirit set Paul apart to accomplish His work. In
the process, he was driven out of a city, stoned as though to
death, shipwrecked, and imprisoned.

Why would God contrive such things? It is really quite simple: God loves to promote, nurture, and increase faith. He
takes great joy and pleasure in the one who, upon receiving
the promise and then the reversal, stands fast despite the dark-
est of circumstances, trusting and meditating on God's Word.

In my own life I have noticed that God often stirs me to a
desire to minister in a particular way, making it clear that He
has called. Then I experience setbacks. There have been times
when I have turned away and not received the blessing, but

more and more I find myself standing fast, waiting with eagerness for the realization.

There are many areas of our lives where we may see this principle at work, for there are many promises that God has given every believer. Take, for example, our children. "Train up a child in the way he should go. Even when he is old he will not depart from it" (Prov. 22:6). Without doubt, as we raise our children there are many times when we think we see the reversal of this promise. However, if we stand fast in faith, knowing that the reversal often comes first, we can stand in the midst of calamity with the greatest peace. This is the confidence I see in the prodigal son's father (Luke 15:11–32). He was assuredly vexed by his son's unholy behavior, and yet he possessed quiet confidence in God.

We may experience personal reversals so severe that we believe a promise's fulfillment can never come. Look at what Peter had to experience after he had received this from the Lord: "Blessed are you, Simon Barjona, because flesh and blood did not reveal this to you, but My Father who is in heaven. And I also say to you that you are Peter, and upon this rock I will build My church, and the gates of Hades shall not overpower it. I will give you the keys of the kingdom of heaven"(Matt. 16:17–19). Can you imagine how Peter felt after such a promise from the Son of God? But immediately the reversals began. The same Lord looked at him and said, "Get behind me, Satan," and then, "This night you will deny me." Peter stood as fast as he was able then and later. Beyond it all, Peter did receive the carrying out of the Lord's vow.

Church history is replete with saints who had great adverse episodes in their personal lives, in marriage, in family, in ministry, and in health. They walked by faith and not by sight, knowing that when the promises are finally fulfilled, it is the deeper lessons of faith that occurred along the way that are more highly valued.

What has God promised you; what has He led you to do? Is there a yearning in your heart to minister? Then take heart!

He will accomplish all that you desire once you take the position of yielding to Him in quiet confidence and faith. Do not fear the reversals that bring the problems. Stand fast through them and you will receive, not as a spoiled child, but as a person of faith.

We must come to see that difficulties are an integral part of the formula for growth in every believer's life. Obstacles do not mean that a person is abandoned, nor do they hint that he is lower in importance or any less blessed of God. In fact, such a believer is moving ahead to perform within the realm of a greater calling.

> Consider it all joy, my brethren, when you encounter various trials, knowing that the testing of your faith produces endurance.
>
> James 1:2–3

> Blessed is a man who perseveres under trial; for once he has been approved, he will receive the crown of life, which the Lord has promised to those who love Him.
>
> James 1:12

3

God's Funnel

Enter by the narrow gate; for the gate is wide, and the way is broad that leads to destruction, and many are those who enter by it. For the gate is small, and the way is narrow that leads to life, and few are those who find it.

Matthew 7:13–14

Jesus indicates that there are two roads that men can follow: the wide path heading to destruction and the narrow way directed toward life. Believers are moved out of the wide path and into the narrow way through what I like to call God's funnel.

When you want to fill a narrow-necked bottle with water from a large pan, a funnel concentrates and forces the liquid into the small opening precisely where you want it, without wasting a bit.

God has a funnel, in a manner of speaking, that allows Him to take you (a very small creature) out of the masses of humanity and place you exactly where He wants you. If you could examine it, you would find that God's funnel is made up of various problems: contrary people, events, circumstances, vexing church situations, financial pressures, failures, thoughts, dysfunctional marriages, poor health, and trying family situations, to name a few. All these problems are calculated to pressure you, the believer, farther and farther into the narrow way that leads to the very presence of God, where problems will no longer be a concern, but prayer, joy, and praise will be the course of the day.

Rejecting the Funnel

Many make the mistake of rebelling against the problems they discover around them rather than submitting to God's purpose. Several attitudes are revealed when believers are surrounded by difficulties. Some, with great effort, begin to struggle against the funnel. They devise all sorts of methods and work to the point of exhaustion, hoping to get rid of whatever is causing so much misery. They have not learned that God does not do anything about problems if we're trying to solve them ourselves.

Since He is the only One capable of resolving the problem, the self-reliant believer is in the terrible predicament of being so confident in his own strength that he cannot allow God to provide the solution. After all, such a believer carries an invisible bag of tricks containing all the methods he has developed to deal with emergencies: control, manipulation, religion, anger, running, depression, resentment, emotional blocking, blame taking, blame giving, and the list goes on. If God allowed one of these tricks to resolve the problem, then He would be putting His stamp of approval on such pathetic tools for living, while at the same time encouraging a person's desire to be self-sufficient. It is important that God not allow the bag of tricks to help the believer overcome.

It is easy to spot those who are experiencing a failure of their bag of tricks, for they will become angry, withdrawn, and depressed and often will return to the old sins of the past in the hope that these will give some measure of relief. If they experience even the faintest shadow of the lessening of discomfort, they will once again be working full force on the problem with their satchel. In fact, these believers have a need to be cured from what is in reality a state of idolatry; an idol simply being that to which a person runs, apart from God, when in the midst of problems. These idols are varied and can include such things as eating, arguing, withdrawing, controlling, or hard work. Little bags of tricks reserved for resolving life's problems are in reality nothing more than idols, whose effectiveness God will do nothing to confirm.

We simply do not have the resources within ourselves to overcome our problems and live abundantly. There is one lesson that can be taken from the Pharisees, who possessed the most religious, disciplined, and educated of self-lives. Yet they rejected God Himself when they came face to face with Him and are proof that the flesh is of no value in attempting to resolve conflict.

Some become so accustomed to problems that they actually decide this is all that life holds for them. They may complain about their distress, bemoan and lament over their problems, but in all their actions and talk they reveal that they are prepared to remain in this miserable state, for they believe that life in the funnel is all they will ever experience. Remember that the purpose of God's funnel is to bring us through and into His presence. There is no reward for staying miserable our whole lives! We must allow each circumstance to drive us into the presence of God, where we will find our relief.

When he sees the hand of God in the midst of turmoil, a quiet confidence overcomes a believer. This is different from becoming comfortable in the midst of misery, which for many becomes an attitude filter through which the world and others are seen. Once a believer decides that his or her lot in life is to be miserable, every event seems to confirm his theory.

I often see this attitude filter in marriages. The enemy works to convince one of the partners that there is no hope for the marriage. Once this lie is accepted, anything said to that partner hits the filter and is distorted to confirm the lie that the marriage is never going to get any better.

Imagine a factory placed within your head, your ears representing two large doors, one for shipping and the other for receiving. What is manufactured in this factory is misery. If a load of misery is dropped off at the receiving door, it is processed in the factory and comes out the shipping door as refined misery. This causes no surprise whatsoever. What is interesting, however, is that when roses are dropped off at receiving and put through the factory, they too come out as misery. There is something taking place out of sight within the factory that can transform a rose into misery, a kiss into misery, or love into misery.

I often find the misery factory at work in fathers, revealed through their anger over very insignificant events, such as a garden hose left in the yard, a bicycle parked in the middle of the garage, or a job left half-done. In a marriage, anger can arise from a misplaced object, financial pressure, a sharp word, or a task left untouched. At the work place, anger might be generated from the rude co-worker, the lack of satisfaction in the present job description, or even an occupied parking place.

Many men between the ages of thirty and forty find themselves unsatisfied. Some refer to this as the mid-life crisis, wherein a man begins to fear that his life is reaching a point at which fulfillment of his hopes, dreams, and desires is not possible. The man is really angry at himself for his own inability to realize his dreams, but all of this has allowed the enemy to build a misery factory within, causing the man to lay the blame on the wife and children for burdening him with the responsibility of having to provide through a job that he thoroughly hates. The reasoning is as follows: "If my wife and children are the cause of my wretchedness, they should be cast aside or at least be the focus of all my frustration." With the misery factory in full operation, the man cannot accept his wife, his chil-

dren, his job, and the circumstances in which he finds himself
with a joyful and thankful heart. He is unable to see that God
gave the wife, the children, and the job and that to be angry
at these is really to be angry with God.

We must realize that what we consider to be abundant and
worthwhile life will rarely be what God considers valuable. Accepting with joy and thankfulness where we are today as coming from the hand of a loving God, who knows exactly what
we need, allows us to find peace. Once we develop the attitude that everyone is against us, all events seem to prove that
life is miserable, God is not there, and nothing will ever change.
In fact, some of us will even subconsciously structure circumstances just to prove our false theory; believing we are worthless and unwanted, we set out to act in such a way that others
will avoid or overtly reject us.

There are those who actually like their problems and, for
fear that they will lose them, never intend to submit to Christ.
Some use mental and emotional problems to milk acceptance
and attention from everyone and maintain center stage at all
times.

Once I visited a man who was placed in a mental institu-
tion and diagnosed as incurable. His parents told me that even
though they continued to visit him regularly, their son no
longer knew anyone and could not "process" anything that
was said to him. After spending a few minutes with the young
man, I told him that I didn't believe he was sick at all but was
using the whole situation to control the family. At that he became quite angry and vehemently began to argue with me that
he was, in fact, quite sick. I found his ability to argue interesting in light of the family's certainty that he couldn't carry on
a simple conversation.

Believers abound who show mercy to the hurting, as they
should. Unfortunately, often they attract those who have no
intention of getting over their problems and into the presence
of God, but who want to consume as much of the loving believers' time as they can.

Surrendering to the Funnel

Why are we suffering? Why has God not yet delivered us? Why has He yet to change this impossible person or position? Could it be that He has not completed the work in us that the circumstances and situation are to bring about? Could it be that we are not yet despairing of our own idols to deliver us? Could it be that we have yet to surrender to the funnel?

Look at it this way. Imagine taking a twelve-month course entitled "Driven into His Presence." You have suffered much to complete nine months of the course and now are complaining about how difficult it is. God could deliver you out of the classroom; if He did, the nine months in the course would be wasted, and you would have to take it over at a later date. Is that what you really want, for your suffering to be for nothing and to be repeated at a later date? Never! Stay put until it is completed.

One brother told of how when he was a young boy in Brazil, he had always wanted a puppy without a tail. One day his father brought him the coveted puppy, the only problem being that it had a tail. He approached his father about the dilemma and was handed a pocketknife and told, "Go cut it off on a fence post." The youngster took the puppy out, but as he contemplated the situation he felt sorrow, not wishing to cause the pup pain. He still wanted a dog without a tail and decided on an answer that seemed quite logical to a young mind. Instead of causing great discomfort by cutting off the whole tail at once, he would provoke less suffering by cutting it off a little at a time!

You see, many people refuse the pain of the moment, along with the possibility of getting it all over with, and opt for extended pain. Each person must allow those problems God has personalized for him to drive him into His presence. If God is truly loving, He will not deliver anyone before the work is complete.

It used to frustrate me when we would move to a new city and I'd begin to look for a job. "Why, God, when You know the job You have for me, do You make me continue to search? Can't You simply lead me to the right place without all this seeking?" No! He could not show me the job until I had given up on all my efforts and strengths (idols) that I felt I could utilize to secure employment. God must put us in situations that will cause us to give up on ourselves, and then He will provide the answer, which is Himself. Jesus is *the* answer from which originates *an* answer for every situation; when we have Him, very little else is needed.

Do you remember that the men hanging on crosses next to Christ's cross had to have their legs broken? When the Romans crucified someone, they would drive a spike through the person's feet, and if he had enough willpower, he could push his weight down on those spikes, though it caused great pain, to avoid suffocation and remain alive longer. That is, through pain the person would prolong his pain.

Isn't this the condition of many? Through self-will, concerned only with what they perceive as their best interests, they are able to prolong the pain of life itself. Christ, on the other hand, was not full of self-will but laid His will at the feet of His loving Father. If the Father had put Him in such a place as crucifixion, Christ would accept it, waiting on and thanking God for the deliverance that was sure to come. He would be raised from the grave, overcoming death.

We too must come to the place of surrender where self-will gives way to God's will. To come to that point we may need some help, just as did the thieves on their crosses. Only when the soldiers saw the pathetic sight of a crucified person trying to maintain his painful existence would they break his legs to put him out of his misery. While there is any strength left the crucified one fights for life; it sometimes takes the action of another to bring about death.

Do you need the legs of your self-life broken? Is your will such that you cannot give up on yourself? Do you need the action of another to put you out of your misery? The Holy Spirit will do just that through circumstances and relationships. Once you give up and accept the death those things help produce, true life—the life of Christ—will soon follow, for the purpose of the funnel is to bring you near to him.

In short, why are you suffering? Because you are not one of the "many called," but one of the "few chosen." You are suffering because God in His love sees you as someone precious and special whom He wants for Himself. Think of it! You out of millions of people have been called to know God in a deeper way. In order for this to happen, you must come to the end of self. Once you see the glory in this, you will praise Him for every event that has helped bring you this far. Surrender to the funnel with its purpose of bringing you near.

God's Assembly Line

There are two predominant methods of discipleship that exist today. One is man's method, analogous to a mold. Molds reproduce objects that look just like themselves. The objects may be attractive, but there are no variations. Each one is exactly like the one that came before. Discipleship can seek to reproduce the person who is doing the discipling with a mold made of various methods that have proven to the caster (discipler) to be of the most value, such as Scripture memorization, witnessing, proper dress, utilizing particular phrases, and displaying coveted talents. The end result is to produce a replica of the discipler. Schools of evangelism may want to create duplicate evangelists; schools of dynamic missions may try to mold dynamic missionaries. The church is cluttered with programs that promise to reproduce in the life of the pupil whatever the author or teacher possesses in such abundance. This is one form of discipleship.

There is another form of discipleship: God's method for creating useful people consists of individualized attention over a period of time. Imagine having two pieces of clay that were both in the form of a square. If you had a group of 150 people and passed one piece of clay around, asking each individual to make whatever impression he wished on it as it passed by, it would be interesting to note how the clay would change as it moved along. Some would squeeze it, completely changing its form; others might make a very light imprint with their thumbs or fingers; and still others might try to form it back into its original shape. When the piece of clay had been circulated all around and placed next to a piece that did not take the journey, could any one person duplicate in the untouched piece the exact imprints of the handled piece? Of course not! The piece that had been passed around was shaped by the successive additions of 150 people.

So it is with God's method of discipleship. We are not formed by a single mold that quickly makes us like everyone else; rather, we are each shaped uniquely.

Picture any believer as a lump of clay in God's hands. He carries the clay through the potter's workshop, which is full of people, some holding hammers, others brandishing problems, others temptations, and some holding bandages. We may be surprised to find that demons are allowed to be in the shop, as well as physical illness. As God holds the lump of clay, he calls out various people and events. Only those God calls out are allowed to step forward to make an impression on the clay. Sometimes it is attacked, and its appearance becomes distorted and ugly. At other times a hidden beauty, never before imagined, begins to emanate from this simple lump of clay. Through the constant pushing, crushing, and shaping, we find something quite useful and very beautiful, a perfect expression of the very heart of the Potter Himself. He has created something for His glory, something to express Him, and something for a very special good work. In the end, the created object is full of life and cannot look back with anger at a single event or person for appearing, at first, to hurt and distort him. Instead, this beautiful creature boasts in the Lord alone, not desiring to create another like himself, but encouraging others to submit to God's hand in order to be made into something useful, beautiful, and unique.

It is interesting that one of the greatest missionaries who ever lived was told not to go to the mission field for he did not possess the needed training. He went, allowing God to develop him into what He wanted. Now there exists a mission school in this man's name, which attempts to mold other great missionaries into his likeness. Yet none have excelled to the stature of the believer in whose honor the training facility was founded. Why? Because this man allowed God to change him from a lump of clay into a useful disciple. A mold created by men can never produce such a masterpiece.

There is no higher call for a believer than to submit to God's work in his life and to encourage others as they do the same. Those who know the potential in a lump of clay are not frantic to throw that clay into a mold and reproduce in another what they deem important. They know the clay must be shaped by God through time. These disciplers are content not to mold, but to make the impression on the clay that God has created and gifted them to make. And when it is their turn to be molded, they receive the marks with joy, knowing they are being changed and developed according to God's will.

Do not see this process as only problems and pain; keep the goal in mind: the beautiful person the Master Craftsman is creating. Be encouraged by what you are becoming: the expression of His beauty and a productive vessel in Him.

Therefore, since we have so great a cloud of witnesses surrounding us, let us also lay aside every encumbrance, and the sin which so easily entangles us, and let us run with endurance the race that is set before us, fixing our eyes on Jesus, the author and perfecter of faith, who for the joy set before Him endured the cross, despising the shame, and has sat down at the right hand of the throne of God.

Hebrews 12:1–2

2
Part

Roadblocks
in the
Narrow Way

Once we conclude that there is no hope of overcoming our problems by ourselves, and once we are driven to God for the solution to our dilemmas, we will move out of God's funnel into the narrow way that leads to His presence. As long as we focus on a problem with all our energies, the enemy is quite content to leave us alone. Once we realize, however, that deliverance must lie in God and begin the journey toward His presence, the enemy develops great concern; the believer who lives in the presence of God is "more than a conqueror." Therefore, the enemy places a series of roadblocks in the narrow way in an attempt to turn back the would-be overcomer.

As I have discipled hundreds of believers in differing countries and cultures, it has been interesting to note that there is a consistency in the roadblocks that the enemy erects in order to hinder believers on their journeys to living out of the power that is theirs before the Father's throne. Let's look now at some of the most common roadblocks.

4

Fears

Fear of Rejection

There are many who understand the need to be near to God yet fear that possibility; they continually live a life of avoidance. Why would anyone not love to spend each day basking in the glow of his Savior? For many, the fear of just such an encounter has its roots in rejection, which has left them with the fear that once they are near God, He too will reject them. The reasoning moves along these lines: "It will hurt when God rejects me; therefore, I will avoid God, hence avoiding the pain of rejection." This fear was revealed in Adam after his sin ("I was afraid . . . so I hid myself") and again in Peter ("Depart from me"). There is, of course, some relevance in this reasoning, for when we have failed others, they have more often than not rejected us. We know we have failed God, so we assume He will reject us. God, however, does not behave as a man and is not to be judged as a man. He who is driving you into His presence is a God of compassion; He will surely not reject you when you arrive.

People will turn away from the homosexual, the prostitute, the controlling woman, the gossip, the drunk, the proud, and the self-righteous, but God does not turn away from them. Although their behavior is sinful, they must understand that God is hurting for them. The compassion of God fills Him with pain when He sees the zenith of His creation living in wretchedness.

Don't think for one moment that when God sees you surrounded with problems and misery, He is not moved by your condition. He will choose to wait and act only when your ultimate good has been served and these circumstances have driven you into His loving arms. The comfort you receive will soothe the memory of those terrible events.

Imagine a bucket in God's possession with your name on it. Each day as you suffer, the bucket is slowly filled with His compassion. At the proper time, when suffering has produced all that God has intended it to, the full bucket will be dumped on you.

I have witnessed this principle at work often in the lives of believers. One afternoon a man entered my office and announced that I really wouldn't be able to help him because he was not a believer. It was obvious from the stress on the man's face that he was in the midst of much turmoil. He shared some of the events of his life, which had been filled with physical, emotional, and mental abuse by a psychopathic father. This man judged God to be just like his earthly father, so it was no wonder that he had no intention of becoming a believer. As I sat there, my spirit became aware that God's bucket of compassion had finally been filled for this man. God would tolerate no more of his suffering. I needed only to open my mouth and share the simplest of Christian truths in order to watch as the man was flooded by the love and compassion of God. The dear brother had been so hurt that he could hardly express any emotion, but I did notice that a small tear ran from his eye. Yes, a very small tear, but it represented for this man the last drop in the bucket, now filled to overflowing. It was over! Problems had served both God and this man. The Lord was now satisfied, having received the man's life, and the man was now satisfied, having received God's life. All this was made possible by problems.

Never allow the enemy to succeed in erecting the roadblock that leads you to believe that once you are in the presence of God, He will treat you as a man treats you, for our God is a God of compassion.

Fear of Total Surrender

Much is written about total commitment to the Lord by the believer. I prefer the word *surrender*. While *commitment* implies that we must do something, *surrender* seems to acknowledge that God, and God alone, can accomplish what is needed. We are as branches surrendered to the vine, trusting Him for all that we need. Our very life must come from Him. Surrender is an attitude, rather than something we must do.

Many fear the total surrender they believe nearness to God will demand; they struggle with wanting to hang onto things they have reserved for themselves and attempted to hide from God. Or in the past they have given God a particular sin or situation and all appeared to remain unchanged. This has led to despair and the conclusion that if anything is to happen, they must make it happen themselves. Those with such experiences have a distorted view of what total surrender really is, for they have associated it with either immediate loss or immediate results.

Several years ago I met a girl who wanted more than anything else to serve the Lord in ministry. There was one problem: she struggled continually with depression. I asked her several questions, such as, "Do you enjoy being despondent?" "Is there any satisfaction that you are receiving from feeling low?" (For many love the sympathy they receive from others and have no intention of living any other way.) I asked if she could identify events that had caused the dejection. Then I turned to the issue of sin in her life. To all my probing she responded with honest and clear answers, and there was no apparent reason for the depression.

I asked her one more question. "Did Christ love His Father in heaven any more when He was on the Mount of Transfiguration, where the disciples beheld His glory, than He did when He was hanging on a cross at Calvary where He was crucified?"

Her answer was correct: "He loved Him no more or no less in either place."

I explained that surrender is loving God in the midst of the bad as well as the good times; it is loving God in the midst of sadness or joy, for He is God. I then told her to make depression the focus and main issue of her life no longer, but to make Christ all. As she stopped worrying about her inability to serve the Lord because of her inadequate emotional health, she soon found herself unwittingly serving Christ without reserve. It didn't happen overnight, but it did happen.

We must love the Lord as much during our most severe trials as we do when we are surprised by pleasant events. There are many believers who want to be totally surrendered to the Lord in order to receive constant blessings, but when events turn painful they grab back the control in order to work everything out themselves, refusing to wait on Him.

Look at Job's attitude of simple surrender; he had determined to stand fast even in the worst of events, circumstances, and problems. "Shall we indeed accept good from God and not accept adversity?" (Job 2:10). No matter what was dealt him, he did not want to waver.

When apparent adversity comes and you resolutely choose to surrender, do not expect others to encourage you in your decision. Remember that Job's wife was not supportive of his position. Do not expect comfort from others; the only solace you will know is that which God gives. You must learn to love the taking up of the cross and the denial of self that constitute total surrender, for that love will allow you to maintain peace in the midst of even Job-like experiences.

If you choose the cross, you will be choosing the Lord Jesus. As you practice surrendering to God in whatever He brings, there will be times when you find the yielding quite easily accomplished with great confidence and strength. At other times it will be in weakness with much struggle, but remember, the important thing is that you do surrender. In weakness or strength, your attitude toward God must always remain that of relinquishing your life with a grateful heart.

I believe that the spiritual man does not see good or bad events, but only God. The enemy works toward our displaying zealous extremes: indulging or neglecting self; working hard to please our mates or giving up and saying, "Who cares?"; clamoring against the ugly manifestations of the flesh while proudly displaying other deeds of the same self-life. The spiritual, surrendered man responds the same to praise and condemnation, weakness and strength, freedom and imprisonment, sweetness and bitterness, temptation and defeat, pain and health, weariness and delight, or uncertainty and a definite plan, for he is Christ-centered and living for Him who is above all that is earthly. He lets nothing delay his course for even a moment. Surrender does not require great strength, but merely the yielding to God's strength and living daily in the awareness and experience of it.

Fear of Being a Sponge

The enemy has persuaded many to believe that if they surrender totally to the Lord, their lives will be filled with abuse and misery as others afflict and use them. Satan gains such a foothold because few believers have learned the blessing that comes from receiving the cruelty that the world casts on them—of being a sponge to those around them.

A sponge is used to absorb. Rather than letting anger, frustration, or bitterness bounce off him to afflict someone else, the believer absorbs it and stops its progress. Anger is like the ball in a tennis match. As each opponent is able to return it, the speed of the ball increases until someone loses. When the manifestations of the self-life are volleyed, there is one major difference: There will never be a winner, for in the Christian life there are no winners, but only "loser/losers" and "loser/winners." When manifesting the flesh, or when another person's flesh is revealed and a believer responds in kind, he is a "loser/loser." If he absorbs the ugliness coming from others, however, he will find that the whole matter can come to a stop. The common lie we fall for is that he has lost, but in reality he has won: He is a "loser/winner," having apparently lost on earth but won in the kingdom of God. Just so, Christ absorbed to the death what mankind dished out, and He has won forever riches, power, honor, and glory. He appeared to be a loser when He was crucified; He is a complete winner.

Are you willing to bring the conflict within your home, within your relationships, and within your own heart to a conclusion? Then simply be a sponge. Throughout the day absorb all that is from the carnality of man around you and watch as the peace of Christ prevails.

Being a sponge is a blessed life, one of true strength and character. "When we are reviled, we bless; when we are persecuted, we endure; when we are slandered, we try to conciliate; we have become as the scum of the world"(1 Cor. 4:12–13). Paul was a man of great fortitude because he was a sponge for those around him.

There are three ways to view the command to love. The first is from the perspective of the law, which teaches, in essence, to love or God will punish you. The second is from the desire to be happy through obedience to Scripture by loving as you love yourself. The third and highest view flows from the life of Christ, which actually enables you to love your enemy. The first is a good way, the second is an excellent way, but the third

is God's perfect way. It is the way of being a sponge, of denying yourself, not the Lord within you.

Once a man came to me concerning his marriage. His wife,
he said, was always saying things that offended him. This man
was very intimidating and forceful. He told me about several
dangerous situations he had been in during his life and how
his determination and strength had brought him through. I
was truly amazed as he spoke of these perilous events, for I
knew that had I been faced with the same situations, I would
not have fared nearly as well as he had. He was truly coura-
geous in every sense of the word. However, when he finished
talking, I responded by calling him a pantywaist and a wimp.
He nearly came out of his chair as he leaned forward and sput-
tered, "Explain yourself!" I could not have participated in his
hazardous undertakings, I said, but the true test of manhood
was not in those things, but in the degree to which we can be
sponges. I told him that it was a pathetic sight to see such a
strong man complaining about some little thing that his wife
said in a manner that did not please him and considering divorce because he could not absorb harsh words. Despite all his
outward ability, he was a weakling.

How many marriages would be immediately transformed
if the husband or wife would consent to being a sponge. It is
the inability to lose that causes the development of so many
roots of bitterness in couples. A man may go to bed, and if his
wife says something that is offensive, he may punish her by not
talking to her. She may retaliate by refusing to touch him. He
then might find new ways to make her pay, and the marriage
spiral descends, all too often as far as divorce. The sad thing is
it could all be stopped by one or the other's simply receiving
the insult and determining to love.

Your response to every negative situation reveals your heart
more than the heart of the person who brought it to you. Do
you love your wife as God has commanded, or do you only
love her if . . . ? Do you respect your husband as the Bible di-
rects, or do you only respect him if . . . ? The "ifs" in your re-

lationship reveal weakness in you and must be surrendered before God will see the need to change your mate.

Surrender—being a loser/winner—is an abundant life to be coveted, not feared. Push this roadblock out of the way as you draw near to God. With the command to deny self God gives all the spiritual strength needed for its fulfillment.

When discipling someone who is angry over what another has done to or said about him, I like to ask, "Are you offended?" Then I state that I'm glad for the affront and hopeful that in the future he will continue to be insulted. Being offended is a crucial ingredient in the Christian's life, for at the point when others' insolence does not bother us, we will know we are living the abiding life. Jesus could have resented the whole crowd on the day that He was crucified; yet, within a short time He gave these transgressors His very life. If we accept the insults of others, we will be able to give those very people our lives. We die in order that they might live (2 Cor. 4:10–12).

When we are disdained, we have two responsibilities: first, to receive it with forgiveness; second, to pull the offending person out of the condition in which they want to offend others.

Would you like to have a book published that listed in alphabetical order all the people you know and the negative statements that you have made about them? Of course not! No one would like such a thing. You would seek to have the book destroyed. When you hear something negative about yourself stated by another, therefore, for his or her sake as well as your own, destroy the information immediately and do not allow it to affect the relationship. After all, you know you have been guilty of the very same thing.

In the midst of every negative confrontation, there is not only something for the angry or injurious person to learn, but something for you, the injured, to learn. Can you forgive, love, and encourage just as the Lord has done for you when you have slighted Him? An offender's heart is readily apparent, but your response reveals your condition, whether of spirit or flesh.

If it is flesh, I hope you will continue to receive affronts until walking in the flesh makes you so miserable that you turn to the deep life within that cannot be offended.

I have often thought how wonderful it would be to attend a church that had posted above its entryway, "This is a congregation of believers who cannot be offended." For I'm often vexed at the way church and staff members intensely scrutinize each other, waiting for shortcomings that will prove their own emotional observations. They critically examine how money is spent, what kind of car is driven, the clothes worn, and even the total square footage of offices, until resentment is stirred up on all sides. These things ought not to be.

If we will take seriously that the Christian life is to be lived in an abiding relationship moment by moment, then we can see each offense as the first of that moment, and therefore the very first one. It is easy to forgive the first trespass, but too many see each one as another drop in the bucket of proof confirming that a person is worthless and should be cut off. By receiving each wrong in the moment, we will find it quite easy to forgive seven times seventy.

Fear of Weakness

Many believe that they are too weak to enter into the presence of God. They have been persuaded that such a privilege is reserved for the mighty. However, weakness is never to be a hindrance.

It was a diverse group of people among the Israelites who went out in the morning to collect the manna. Some were young and strong, while some were old, widowed, or weak. If the strong collected a great amount, they would find the next morning that they actually had no extra. At the same time, the weak, who collected only a small portion, found that they had all they needed. The strong and the weak were treated alike, for God shows no partiality.

So it is with believers who daily collect the true manna (Jesus) that has come down from heaven. Those with great endurance cannot collect any more than those with much deficiency. Again, God shows no partiality. The full life of the Son is available for even the very weakest, who are, in fact, the most suited for a life in the presence of our Savior. For it is in our strength that we will most likely rest comfortably and fail to acknowledge our moment-by-moment need of Him.

The enemy has persuaded many to believe that they are incapable of a deep relationship with the Lord. This deception is possible because of misconceptions about what a deep relationship with the Lord really is. Believers may think it is a monastic life of prayer and religious duty, ministering in a faraway country, or arriving at a level of expressed perfection. When defined in such terms, is it any wonder that few believe such a life is for them? The Lord's definition of a deep life is not burdensome, but one wherein we simply yield our spirits to Him each moment. It is the natural life of abiding, the same effortless awareness possessed by a branch grafted into a vine. While the branch may feel nothing special, there is yet a quiet dependence and confidence in the vine to provide all that is needed. Gazing at a branch, we see that the life it lives in unbroken reliance is not only possible, but is the most natural way for it to exist. In fact, it would be much more difficult and artificial for the branch to live in a vase, cut off from the vine. The deep life of abiding is possible for all, even the very weakest.

How the body of Christ has suffered through the constant comparison of one member with another! Many revivals merely center on a single person, who spends one week recounting all that he has accomplished. Covertly, those sitting in the pew compare themselves to such a one and conclude that they will never be that effective or pleasing to God. The church is then left with many who feel too weak, unprepared, and defeated ever to enter into a deep relationship with the Lord.

It must be made clear that what is needed for the blessed life of unbroken fellowship with the Lord is not superior intellect, ability, or power, but a quality of heart that can easily be determined. Anyone who answers in the affirmative to the question "Do you love Him?" possesses all that is needed for a deep walk with the Lord. We must grasp one simple truth that has been choked out and hidden. Since God gave His Son to obtain us, *there is nothing easier for us to obtain than the moment-by-moment presence and joy of Jesus Christ.* Nothing easier, for it is something that the Father freely gives to all, even the very weakest.

Never allow the enemy to persuade you that you are not suited for the presence of God, that this blessing may be for others but not for you. Heed the command to enter in with boldness. Why are we told to seek Him? Because He can be found! He intends for every believer to find Him. "And you will seek Me and find Me, when you search for Me with all your heart" (Jer. 29:13). "When Thou didst say, 'Seek My face,' my heart said to Thee, 'Thy face, O LORD, I shall seek'" (Ps. 27:8).

We have heard the command, problems are driving us to Him, and we are free to obey. We will seek the Lord Who can be found.

Fear Itself

As we continue the examination of the obstacles that the enemy puts in front of us when we approach the presence of God, we must be aware that if his other deceptive roadblocks fail, he will gladly use the ace up his sleeve—fear.

It is interesting to note that there are two predominant teachings in Scripture concerning fear. The first encompasses all directives to fear God. "You who fear the LORD, praise Him" (Ps. 22:23). "The fear of the LORD is the beginning of wisdom" (Ps. 111:10). "The secret of the LORD is for those who fear Him, and He will make them know His covenant" (Ps. 25:14). "Behold, the eye of the LORD is on those who fear Him, On those who hope for His lovingkindness" (Ps. 33:18).

This first teaching is the groundwork for the second concerning fear. "See, the LORD your God has placed the land before you; go up, take possession, as the LORD, the God of your fathers, has spoken to you. *Do not fear* or be dismayed" (Deut. 1:21). "Then I said to you, 'Do not be shocked, nor fear them'" (Deut. 1:29). "But the LORD said to me, 'Do not fear him, for I have delivered him and all his people and his land into your hand; and you shall do to him just as you did to Sihon, king of the Amorites'" (Deut. 3:2).

Our God is a jealous God! We are to have no other gods before Him. One of the characteristics of a false god is that it inspires fear, without which the worshipers would soon lose interest and go their own way.

It is simple to discern what men worship by observing what makes them apprehensive. Many allow finances to unsettle them, so they have put their trust for provision in money rather than in their heavenly Father. Some approach the authorities with trepidation, revealing their hope (realized or unrealized) in those in power. Some dread the actions of men, for it is in mankind they have placed their expectations. The list goes on. It is important to realize that we are *commanded* to fear nothing but God.

Fear is reserved as one of the highest forms of worship. Satan parades himself as the god of this world and demands the fear of his followers. However, we are commanded to fear only the one true God, the Father of our Lord Jesus Christ. He alone is worthy of the fear of humankind. To give our fear to a god such as Satan is to worship him. This is sin! Our worship of the one true God is meant to free us from every other fear: of Satan, man, or circumstances. "And do not fear those who kill the body, but are unable to kill the soul; but rather fear Him who is able to destroy both soul and body in hell"(Matt. 10:28).

You see why the enemy loves to inspire fear in God's people, for in so doing he proves to himself that he is more than a fallen angel, a defeated foe, and a roaring lion with no teeth. With fear, Satan receives a measure of worship that is to be reserved for God alone and attempts once again to elevate himself to a position equal to that of God.

When Jesus was in the wilderness, Satan tempted Him: "All these things will I give You, if You fall down and worship me" (Matt. 4:9). The word *worship* is simply defined as "giving attention to." Satan was merely saying, "Give me Your attention!" Jesus refused, stating, "Begone, Satan! For it is written, 'You shall worship the Lord your God, and serve Him only'" (Matt. 4:10). Only God is to have our attention.

Unfortunately, there are many believers who have given Satan undue consideration, for not a day passes that they are not consumed with fear of him as they constantly address his schemes and deceptions. It is not at all uncommon to hear more from them about the enemy than about Christ. They have succumbed, albeit unwittingly, to worship of the enemy, but they err, for his power cannot compare in any way to that of our God.

Many times the struggle between good and evil is portrayed by the Taoist symbol of a small circle, half-white and half-black. The colors are positioned in such a way as to rival each other for domain, but as the black gains ground the white loses, and vice versa. Some believers see the earth and heavens in this type of struggle between the forces of darkness and forces of light. However, this is not the case. "In Him was life, and the life was the light of men. And the light shines in the darkness; and the darkness **did not overpower** it" (John 1:4–5 emphasis mine). Light and darkness do not battle with an equal force, for darkness must always give way to the light. Darkness never overpowers the light but merely moves in when the light allows it to by moving out. Light, on the contrary, does vanquish darkness and force it to move out of the way.

Man has yet to invent a "darklight," the opposite of a flashlight, which can penetrate bright daylight with a black beam. No such thing can disturb light, for darkness has no power over or defense against the light. Yet when I stand on a mountaintop in the very blackest part of a night in which no moon or stars are able to exhibit their gleaming illumination, my inexpensive flashlight can split that darkness apart. An expanse of darkness cannot overcome my cheap little flashlight, but must give way to its beam.

What would our lives be like without the dawn, which immediately forces out darkness and allows for the productivity and security of the day? In our hearts, God's light must arise each day, and all darkness, including fear, will disappear. We need not examine volumes in an effort to understand the darkness and its power when all that is needed is a comprehension of the presence of Christ's light within our hearts. No amount of demonic work will stand against it, for all shadows must flee and make room for its glory.

Just as light is inexpressibly greater than darkness, God's power is infinitely greater than the enemy's. We know, then, that Satan's darkness will only be permitted to operate where God determines it can. It is important that our focus be kept on His light released within, which will force out any darkness that might want to intrude on us.

Satan had to ask permission to do anything at all to Job. Also, in Jesus' words to Peter, "Simon, Simon, behold, Satan has demanded permission to sift you like wheat," we see that Satan was still having to ask before he could go through with his plan, which was allowed by Jesus for a reason: "But I have prayed for you, that your faith may not fail; and you, when once you have turned again, strengthen your brothers" (Luke 22:31–32). Peter, like any of us, would have been doomed without the intercession of the great Light who is Jesus Christ. Without question we need awareness of the enemy's activity, but more importantly we need a heart knowledge of the true omnipotence of our God, whom we worship with fear.

A young woman in the midst of marital conflict with a husband who was quite irrational told me she was always struck with fear whenever she ventured into her basement. I asked her to go to that room, open the Bible, and read the following verses. "And He said to them, 'I was watching Satan fall from heaven like lightning'" (Luke 10:18). "Put on the full armor of God, that you may be able to stand firm against the schemes of the devil" (Eph. 6:11). "Submit therefore to God. Resist the devil and he will flee from you" (James 4:7). "The LORD rebuke you, Satan!" (Zech. 3:2). I suggested that she also order all demonic forces to leave her home, in the name of the Lord Jesus. I cautioned her that if she sensed more fear after she had commanded Satan to leave, it would be important for her not to run from it, for that is the last weapon the enemy uses to make a believer back down. Our fear, therefore, is not evidence of the enemy's power but is the proof that he has no authority to stay. The purpose in the exercise, I told her, was not that she run around looking for demons behind every closet door and under the beds, but that she might recognize the power that is in the light of God.

The next week she returned to my office elated by what had happened. She had been in the basement holding their newborn, and when she began to read the Scriptures, fear enveloped her. Next, she commanded that the enemy leave; the fear became so great that she fell to her knees. She remembered that fear is proof of the enemy's losing power and his all-out attempt to stay, so she stood fast in the victory already won by the blood of Jesus and once more commanded the enemy to leave. Immediately there was a flood of peace in the room.

She said that since that worked so well, she went to stand at the threshold of the front door and commanded Satan never to enter the house again with her husband. Something very interesting took place that night, for her husband would not enter the house to accuse and argue with her. Instead, he wanted her to go out and quarrel with him in his truck. When he came back into the house, he did not want to continue the bickering. "And the God of peace will soon crush Satan under your feet. The grace of our Lord Jesus be with you" (Rom. 16:20).

Happy are those who distrust themselves, putting no confidence in the flesh, but trust the Light who has overcome darkness. We are without a doubt no match for the enemy; however, he is no match for the Light dwelling within us. "But you are a chosen race, a royal priesthood, a holy nation, a people for God's own possession, that you may proclaim the excellencies of Him who has *called you out of darkness into His marvelous light*" (1 Peter 2:9 emphasis mine).

5

Faulty
Definitions

There are many believers who seek spiritual realities in their
lives and never find them. They are sincere and lack no zeal for
or commitment to the project. Why can't all believers find what
is rightfully theirs in Christ? The answer, more often than not,
is found in improper definitions of that for which they search.
The believers' definitions of what they seek and God's definitions of what He gives are not the same, so they are seeking
for something that God does not intend to give. They (or others for them) have defined incorrectly what it means to be spiritual, to be pleasing to God, to be near to God, to be one with
their mates, or to have assurance that they will go to heaven.

Imagine having financial problems and being told that a
yard full of gold is the answer. Having had no previous exposure to gold, you ask, "What does gold look like?" You are told
that a telephone pole is gold. Operating under this false definition, you busy yourself filling the backyard with poles, believing they are the answer to your problems. Then you dis-

cover that all of your labor has been in vain, and you find yourself the poorer for the search.

Having improper definitions has caused much misery in many lives. In the marriage relationship, both husband and wife possess an intangible dictionary of the heart. If I were to draw on my dictionary to define the word *clean,* the following would appear: *clean*—to have a path through the debris from one room to the other. However, if I were able to peek at the same word in my wife's heart dictionary, I would find this: *clean*—see immaculate; opposite of my husband. As you can see, there is a great difference between my definition of *clean* and my wife's.

Another definition that would be interesting to look at would be that of the word *love,* for in my dictionary it would be described as constant holding, kissing, and overt displays of affection; while my wife's definition would include doing good for another, such as cleaning, washing, and cooking meals. The differences in our definitions could cause considerable division. I might say to my wife, "You are not loving me" (I want her to be involved in more emotional activities), and her response may be, "*You* are not loving *me*" (she would like me to do more helpful, physical activities). The truth is that we may both be loving each other as much as we can according to our own definitions; however, we have not loved each other much at all according to the other's definition. We just haven't understood what the other wants or means when attempting to receive or give love.

We can all readily see how much unmerited conflict is caused for couples because of their differing definitions. This conflict can go so far as to drive mates to give up on each other as each one concludes that the other will never change.

Relating to our mates with differing definitions also causes our perceptions of them to be distorted. Imagine a very emotional husband who loves heights standing on top of the Empire State Building, and on the street below the very analytical, unemotional wife who fears heights. If the husband were to move three floors down from the top, would he appear any closer to the wife below? Of course not! Even though the husband has made an improvement in his position, she can perceive none. Her comment could well be, "I still can't see you!" Then the husband, recognizing that his change was not appreciated, might believe he could just as well return to the top, where he had been comfortably enjoying the scenery. On the other hand, under great stress and fear, the wife could move up three floors and begin to wave at her husband, certain that he will appreciate her very difficult attempt to get near to him. His response would be, "I can't see you; aren't you coming up?" That is all the discouragement the wife would need to return immediately to her comfort zone, the ground. They are no closer to each other than they were at the beginning, and now they refuse to make further attempts to draw near.

If we could understand our mates' definitions and perceptions, we could be encouraged and also support their efforts. This is rarely the case, however.

If we are the bride of Christ, does it not follow that He has a dictionary containing all the definitions concerning our life together? That dictionary is represented by the Scriptures. We, too, have our own heart dictionaries concerning our relationships with Him. The question is, do His definitions and ours match up? If not, we will find ourselves living very unfulfilled, dissatisfied lives, perceiving that we are complete failures and utterly unacceptable to God.

I like to give defeated believers a spiritual perception test. The questions are as follows:

How do you know with certainty that God hears?

How will you know when you are near to God?

How will you know that you have become spiritual?

How will you know when God accepts you?

How will you know when you are pleasing to God?

How will you know when you are free from your sin?

How will you know when your life counts for God?

How will you know when you are holy?

What is abundant life?

What must you do to gain rewards?

Few pass the test. Why do the majority of believers possess God's definitions (Scripture) yet not believe them? They continue to search for the things of God using their own inadequate, faulty meanings. One example is with the question "How will you know that you are near to God?" Answers to this often indicate certain attitudes or feelings about nearness. According to God's definition in Psalm 139, there is no place to hide from His presence; we are always near to Him! The nearness itself need evoke no feelings, because it is something that is received by faith, not sight. We are near because God says we are; when we believe this, we know it is an awareness, not a feeling to be sought. If we continue to search for what we already possess, it will elude us.

I met a man who believed that the only place on the planet where oxygen existed was in his own living room. While visiting my office he was frantic (because he thought there was no oxygen there) and angry (it was my fault he had to leave the place where he could breathe). What a pathetic sight, a man gasping and looking for air in a room full of it, all because he had believed a deceiving voice that had him convinced if the room were really full of oxygen, some special feeling would overcome him in confirmation. The poor man only needed to stop, rest, and take a deep breath.

Such is the believer who continues to look for the nearness of God according to his own definitions, not knowing that since he possesses Christ, he possesses God's nearness. Is there anyone closer to God than Christ? The believer need look no further but can begin to live a life near to God! He may feel nothing, but faith is not feeling. As he rests and takes a deep breath of the Lord, he will know that he has always had that for which he sought. "For in Him we live and move and exist" (Acts 17:28).

A faulty definition that can greatly hinder a Christian is the confusion over what constitutes abiding in Christ. In order to shed some light on this issue, it is helpful to examine what the abiding life is not.

First, the abiding life is not getting along with everyone. Even though we have been commanded to love others, how that love is received does not accurately show whether we are carnal or spiritual. Christians sometimes think that their maturity is subtly measured by the responses of others. That is, if people they love respond positively, then they are spiritual; any negative reactions show their immaturity. Many suffer under self-condemnation and the judgments of others when they do not have an effectual relationship with parents, mates, neighbors, or work associates. Jesus clearly taught, however, that if men hated Him, they would hate us, that He brought a sword to divide, and that even families would be destroyed because of Him. "And brother will deliver up brother to death" (Matt. 10:21). This is not to give any excuse for believers' carnal behavior, but it must be pointed out that Christians will be persecuted, disliked, slandered, and blamed when they have done little or nothing to bring it about. Paul asks if light and darkness can fellowship together. Some in darkness are seeking the light, and these we must guide; but some love the darkness and hate those in the light, and sometimes these turn out to be family members.

Some think that a Christian must beware when someone thinks ill of him, since this is an indication that he is in some kind of error. Jesus said the exact opposite in Luke 6:26: "Woe to you when all men speak well of you, for in the same way their fathers used to treat the false prophets."

Even when we do not get along with other believers, we are not necessarily carnal, selfish, and sinful. Nor is there the implication that we should not be ministering. John Wesley became a tremendous man of God, but he simply could not get along with his own wife; she refused to live in harmony. He did not stop loving her, but neither did he take all the blame and cease to minister.

On one occasion, as I prepared to direct a seminar on living the abiding life, a pastor continued to bring to my attention all the minute doctrines he held dear that I might not properly deal with as I taught. Therefore he was not sure he could associate himself with the meetings. I simply stated that I understood his objections and why he could not participate. I also explained that the conference was not for everyone; it need not draw those who were well and victorious, but those who struggled. He then accused me of being arrogant for not wanting to argue about our minor differences.

A brother from England spoke on the deeper life in Christ and afterward was confronted by a disgruntled listener wanting to know his position on predestination. My friend listened as his view was disputed and then responded with, "Excuse me, what did you say about Jesus?"

The contentious one retorted, "I wasn't talking about Jesus; I was talking about predestination," and continued his diatribe.

My friend listened patiently and at length again asked, "Excuse me, what did you say about Jesus?"

In frustration, the man exclaimed, "I wasn't talking about Jesus! I'm trying to discuss predestination!"

At that, my friend responded, "I can no longer talk to you, for I only want to talk about what is important . . . Jesus."

The point is that the deeper life may include conflict with others. In every case, we must always remain grounded in love, for the one not loving is a rebel in God's kingdom. But we must not be sidetracked from our walk by those who refuse to get along with us.

In fact, when some family members, work associates, and church members speak ill of us, they are actually giving us a compliment! For their behavior, obvious to all, is quite carnal: contentious, angry, bitter, and controlling.

Second, the abiding life does not mean that we never make mistakes, because these are made even by deeply spiritual and devout believers. My grandfather at different times has raised both sheep and pigs. It is interesting to note that after a rain, sheep—usually from stupidity—can end up in the middle of the feed lot up to their bellies in mud, with all four feet stuck beyond mobility. In that condition, they immediately begin to bleat for help. They have put themselves in a ridiculous situation, which they are helpless to remedy. On the other hand, when the pigs get loose, they purposely head for the mud hole, and once they find themselves up to their bellies in the muck, they roll and revel in it, fully happy to be there. If you try to pull them out, they loudly object with squeals.

Believers who are experienced in the abiding life do, like the sheep, sometimes—again, out of stupidity—find themselves in the muck of sin. However, unlike carnal believers who roll in it and enjoy their condition, the spiritual believers will begin to cry for help, not enjoying the place where they have put themselves. Yes, believers deep in their walks with Christ do fail, they do stupid things, they may succumb to sin, but they never, never enjoy it.

A Hindu once said that religion was victory, victory, victory. That is what religion attempts to proclaim and give, a one-time fix. However, Christianity is not religion; rather, it is the Way, the Truth, and the Life. Once we come to Christ, the life that enters us often does so with such force and joy that we may find ourselves shocked that anything of the old nature remains. Yes, the old person has been crucified, removed, and is no longer there. However, the baggage of the old person remains. The spiritual believer must then learn the secret of taking up the cross daily and denying the baggage of the old nature. The spiritual believer's life could most accurately be characterized as defeat, defeat, victory; or defeat, victory, defeat; or even possibly victory, victory, defeat. Christ's life continues to expand within and to reveal more that He will take away. Never become discouraged with failures that come, for the fact remains we do have a victorious life within that will express itself.

Third, the abiding life does not mean that we are not tempted. Temptations do not reveal the heart of the one tempted but the character of the tempter, the enemy. Too many Christians are obsessed by their temptations. They worry about what kind of believers they must be to have such thoughts. The very fact that they wonder at the temptations, however, is proof these are not representative of their true characters.

Where do believers receive these faulty definitions that exercise more power over them than God's definitions? More often than not, they come from the concerns held important by the believers' Christian subcultures (denominations or groups). These emphases, usually rooted in significant experiences and accomplishments of the leading proponents within the group rather than from scriptural fact, will, with the passing of time, become dogma, confused with spiritual realities but not questioned by the members.

For example, when smoking a cigar was a symbol of prominence, some noted evangelists would hold a cigar in their hands while they preached. Currently in this country, smoking a cigar is considered to be a non-Christian thing to do; the person who smokes is seen as less acceptable to God than the believer who has never smoked or who has overcome the habit.

Christian subcultures exercise a tremendous influence on their adherents, defining for them what true spirituality is. Memorizing Scripture, not watching television, attending every church service, never taking an alcoholic drink, not dancing or playing cards, having emotional displays of revelations, or even staying calm in the midst of a great moving of the Spirit are some traits of spiritual people as defined in certain circles.

Once while traveling in Africa I attended two churches that were founded by the same American teacher, who has a very distinctive preaching style. To my amazement, both pastors, having been trained by this man, walked, talked, held their Bibles, and used phrases in the same way as their teacher. For them, his outward behavior had become the mark of true spirituality; they were now striving to imitate him, and should they fail in their actions, they believed they would have failed at being spiritual. As they demonstrated this behavior to their congregations, the younger believers must have thought that this is how a true man of God walks, talks, and holds his Bible. At this point, their subculture is exercising more power over them than the Scriptures.

Where have your definitions for successful spirituality come from? From others, from your church subculture, from your own experiences? The important thing is that they agree with God's, for you may be stopped in your journey to His presence because of false ideas and perceptions concerning your life in Christ. You may be looking for what you already possess! Most of the Christian life is not elusive, but is there to be received. Stop and learn the true character of God, and searching will be replaced by praising.

God's definitions for success can be found in the Sermon on the Mount, for there we see what the children of God express through their new nature—Christ's life within. This unique expression of heavenly living sets the believer apart from the world. Church creeds, doctrinal statements, and systematic theologies can be believed wholeheartedly and yet leave the adherents unchanged. There is enough dynamite in Matthew 5 to blow away all remnants of self when Christ's life is released through a Christian in moment-by-moment fellowship with Him. A misunderstanding of many believers is that a coveted one-time fix exists, and afterwards, by a supernatural act of the Holy Spirit, they will find themselves living in constant unhindered victory. Israel collected the manna in the wilderness. If they collected more than enough for one day, it turned wormy. Jesus is the true manna, and the Jesus you had yesterday is not good for today. He is gathered, so to speak, daily. God is not satisfied with a one-time fix, a one-time filling, nor a one-time deliverance. God wants us in an abiding relationship where we acknowledge every day that apart from Him we can do nothing. Abiding is heavenly living on earth, a life of receiving moment by moment what is needed from a loving Father.

Misplaced Priorities

The Christian's own subculture affects him in another way. It can help him develop priorities that may not be God's priorities. If I order priorities from one to ten, what I consider to be a ten may merely be a one to God, and vice versa. There exists, then, the possibility of going through life working on what I feel are tens and missing God's true tens.

For example, many believers have one sin in their lives that they believe must be banished before they can be pleasing to and effective for God. To them the sin is a ten on the scale. For some, the sin is homosexuality, causing them not to address any other issues in the Christian life until this sin is removed. However, for God the sin of homosexuality is not a ten; it may be a one. One of God's tens is that we abide in the Son (John 15) moment by moment, the reason being that as we abide, we receive as our own Christ's life, which is free from sin. If a person works to overcome homosexuality in his own strength and through discipline, the end result will be a heterosexual who is still not abiding and heeding God's ten.

I have often commented that God has delivered me from many things, but not once has he delivered me from something I was working to overcome. Deliverance is natural once we have our priorities straightened out and are keeping His tens, which in and of themselves bring freedom.

Let God define for each of us what is a ten. Too often we fall short, thinking God's tens are buildings, baptisms, budgets, patching up relationships, examining every area of our lives, and getting others to admit the wrong they have done to us. Are these really God's tens?

Recently, after attending a program professing to spur participants on toward spirituality, I returned home perplexed at how difficult it can be to live as a Christian. I decided to search the Scriptures to discover how many of the tens presented at the conference were actually God's tens. I thought, rather than looking at all we are to do, I would focus on a more serious topic: the things we are never to neglect. I found five things that are never to be neglected (God's tens): prayer and sharing the good news, Acts 6:2–4; our spiritual gifts, 1 Timothy 4:14; so great a salvation, Hebrews 2:3; showing hospitality, Hebrews 13:2; and doing good and sharing, Hebrews 13:16. To my amazement, not one of God's tens was featured during the program that claimed to teach how to be a dynamic, successful Christian.

The Christian life is a simple one to live; it must be, for it is the very weakest and most childlike who are best suited for it. However, the enemy has encouraged the development of many a thick discipleship notebook to turn away the would-be victorious believer from the simplicity of the Gospel.

The Unknown Will of God

How would you like to know the will of God with certainty and great ease? Most would answer in the affirmative, for they earnestly seek the perfect will of God in their lives and fear that they will not find it. They find themselves bogged down in the tedious job of finding something that they cannot define but readily acknowledging they do not possess. The enemy handily sidetracked them from their course of coming into the presence of God.

I remember when a friend came to me after taking a trip to Europe. This man was quite upset with God, since although he had taken the trip at God's leading, things had not developed as he had hoped. The first thing that my friend said was, "You know I went to Europe just as God told me to."

My immediate response was, "Yes, I recall your telling me that God had told you to go to Europe. However, I don't believe that God did specifically tell you to go; you went to Europe because you wanted to go. You only said He told you to go so none of us would argue with you. Isn't that so?" My friend admitted that he did in fact want to go and that God had not specifically told him to go. My next question was, "What's wrong with going to Europe if you want to go? Does God really care where you take your vacation?" You see, it really doesn't matter if you go to Europe or not. Let me explain.

What exactly is the will of God? In Psalm 40:8 David said he delighted to do the will of God. In Matthew 6:10 we are commanded to pray that His will be done on earth. And Mark 3:35 says, "For whoever does the will of God, he is My brother and sister and mother." We all want and seek the perfect will of God, but the facts would seem to indicate that few have actually found it. There are few believers who will confidently say, "I am in the perfect will of God." Why? So few possess the exact will of God because they have wrongly decided what the will of God is and therefore are not looking for the right thing. They may have determined that the will of God is a particular vocation, person, school, ministry, or material object. The will of God is not a person, place, or thing, and as long as the will of God is seen as such it will be missed.

What, then, is the will of God? It is the condition of having a heart that can be led. The will of God is the attitude in a person's walk throughout the day (Eph. 5:15–21; Rom. 12:2–3), not the specifics of where he might go. Jesus possessed this heart attitude: "My food is to do the will of Him who sent Me" (John 4:34). The will of God, quite simply, involves the willingness to always be led by Him. "I have found David the son of Jesse, a man after My heart, who will do all My will" (Acts 13:22).

Many have the cart before the horse, believing that their main efforts in life must be spent discerning the tasks the Lord has for them rather than turning their hearts toward God. Once the heart condition is resolved, the doing of the specific will of God comes quite naturally. We are not to have our focus on the task but on Him who leads us to the task.

The apostle Paul is the perfect example of a man in the will of God, for Paul had set his heart to be led of God. He first received a call concerning *how* to live his life: "to testify solemnly of the gospel of the grace of God" (Acts 20:24). Once he received this call, we read that Paul *decided* where to go, and wherever he *decided* to go was in the will of God (Acts 15:36–41).

Paul was always willing to change direction, demonstrating his acceptance of being led. As Paul traveled, determining where to go, at one point "the Spirit of Jesus did not permit them" (Acts 16:7). Paul simply passed by that place and continued making up his mind as to where he ought to work. Soon after that, he received a vision directing him to Macedonia, and he obeyed because his heart was right. After the work in Macedonia was completed, Paul did not stop and wait for another vision but continued making decisions regarding his journey.

In Paul we see the progression of walking in God's will. He did not have to wear himself out choosing what to do, for it was God's responsibility to redirect if necessary. Again, the will of God is not an activity, but the inclination of the heart in executing the activity. With a right heart, whatever a person does is the perfect thing. There is no distinction between secular and Christian work; there are only secular and Christian hearts.

Jesus, we are told, is the Good Shepherd. On the other hand, we are His sheep, whose duty is following. The responsibility to lead and to take us where we ought to go belongs to God. It is His job to know where we are going, to bring us back if we get off track, and to seek us if we are lost. Do you see the beauty of letting God be God? Your only obligation is to have a heart willing to be led, and you will always be in the will of God.

Was my friend right in his decision to go to Europe? Was he in the will of God? Yes, as long as he possessed a right heart. How can you know if you possess such a heart? Your responses to two basic questions will tell you. If Jesus spoke to you audibly and told you to do something, would you obey? Second, if Scripture speaks against a course of action, would you turn away from it? (For example, a believer who is contemplating marrying an unbeliever should be restrained by scriptural directive.) If you answered yes to both questions, then you can vacation wherever you wish, marry whomever you choose, minister wherever you want, and accept any vocation you like. Since you have a right heart, it is the responsibility of Jesus to direct your steps. Each morning as you walk in your decisions, simply acknowledge, "If the Lord wills, [I] shall live and also do this or that" (James 4:15).

Once a young woman asked me if she should marry her boyfriend. She didn't know if it was the right thing to do. He was a believer, they prayed together, and she loved him. She was so happy with the prospect of the marriage that maybe her own selfish desires were in the way of what God wanted. Was it God's perfect will? How would she know? The questioning went on and on. Finally I said, "You don't have a God, do you?" She quickly said that she did, but once again I said that she did not. I then explained: "Isn't Jesus our Shepherd? Isn't it His job to protect, feed, shelter, seek for the lost, and make sure that His sheep hear His voice?" She answered yes. "Then why are you taking over God's jobs? We have a God; now live as though we have one. Go and marry the man."

You see, the Christian life is simple to live! Do not passively sit around waiting for a voice to direct you. Christ dwells in you; He is the Good Shepherd. You were created for good works; so act. With a right heart, you will not make a mistake.

Dry Times

There is one thing dreaded by many believers: times of dryness in their relationship with the Lord. It is during these times of dryness that the enemy will often step up his attack and hurl hundreds of doubting questions into believers' minds, making them challenge even their own salvation. It is essential to realize that dry times are an integral element of our growth and have a purpose that is very precious. As we press on in Christ, we must see that these experiences are normal for growing believers.

A tree reveals its greatest beauty during spring. Soon afterward the flowers are replaced by fruit; then the tree slowly experiences the draining of its life into the deepest part of its being, the roots. And then—sometimes overnight—it happens: winter strikes. The tree may feel as though it will die, which it might if not for the fact that the killing cold cannot reach the deepest part of its being. Seemingly ever so slowly, spring returns, and the cycle continues.

Just as for the tree, winter of the soul is a normal part of the believer's life and is crucial to growth. The notion that winter indicates there is something wrong with us is a counterproductive misunderstanding.

Why do we have such high times with the Lord, when we feel His presence, read Scripture, pray, and even preach with no effort at all—and then drought seems to strike? It is because God does not want our relationship with Him to be based on something as nebulous as feelings. Thus, He takes away the frills and festivities of our inner lives.

What a believer is during times of dryness reveals his true spiritual condition; if he continues in prayer, in seeking the Lord, and in operating out of the Lord's presence (even though he feels none), then this believer proves to be a spiritual man. Do we seek God for Himself alone, or are we seeking Him for what we can receive? Are we content to live in His presence because He says we have it, or do we attempt to generate His presence through certain feelings?

In marriage, dry times prove the commitment of one mate to the other. When there are no feelings of oneness in the marriage, and yet both are committed in love to the union and to being one, the bond will *always* be strengthened.

So it is with our Lord. If in spite of feelings we stand fast, our relationship will be strengthened in the end. Dry times never reveal a movement away from us by God, for He always remains the same, which is near to us. Dry times are a normal and necessary element in the believer's life, and we give thanks to Him for what they accomplish in us. We will not listen to the enemy's lie that since we lack feelings, we have been rejected and therefore must *do* something in order to continue our journey.

The Immediate-Results Syndrome

Often we allow our eyes to drift from Christ to our problems and circumstances through the immediate-results syndrome, which defines our success wholly by what we are currently experiencing, whether positive or negative. This syndrome is actually a major obstacle to faith.

Let me illustrate. Most will agree that the United States is losing its economic edge because Americans, unlike those of an oriental mind-set, are not willing to invest in something that will not produce immediate benefits. We want wealth right away, while they are willing to invest year after year, receiving fewer tangible rewards now but knowing that in the future they will be repaid tenfold their original investment. The wait will have been very worthwhile. Having seen the wisdom in investing and waiting, they are not discouraged by an occasional disruption in the current financial situation.

Wanting immediate results is a hindrance to faith; in fact, this mind-set will actually nullify faith. The depth of our faith is not to be judged by how much we have received, but rather by how long we can wait and receive nothing. Faith makes my Christian walk a joy; therefore, if I have voided faith through wanting immediate results, I have also to the same extent annihilated joy.

When believers do not have a long-term plan, they become susceptible to the ups and downs of daily life. Their energies are focused on resolving right away whatever is placed in front of them so they can feel comfortable and secure in the moment. Next they become controllers, pushing God out of the way and trying to fix in their own strength, with a variety of plans and manipulations, what they perceive to be the real problem. These believers simply begin to play God. To say the least, this makes the Christian life a struggle, filled with discouragement, depression, anger, and doom. This causes minds and emotions to be flooded by the enemy with questions, accusations, and feelings of hopelessness. It's tough to play God!

Imagine sitting in a bathtub full of water and having somebody dump into the tub a bucket of Ping-Pong balls on which are written all the problems, circumstances, failures, and people that are causing you trouble. Your job is to somehow keep every ball under water. The whole exercise would at first be exhausting and in the end quite frustrating. This pictures, of course, the believer who is trying in his own strength to control every area of his life.

Now all this is related to one simple Scripture: "But I am afraid, lest as the serpent deceived Eve by his craftiness, your minds should be led astray from the simplicity and purity of devotion to Christ" (2 Cor. 11:3). Is the Christian life simple? Is the answer to living alone, living with others, raising children, not having children, and every other struggle simple? Yes, yes, and yes again! In order for the Christian life to be one of simplicity, we must first realize that God does not give answers to every situation but rather reveals appropriate attitudes for every situation. If these attitudes are maintained, we will not be free from the day-by-day ups and downs, but we will

see the fulfillment of the promises in God's fullness of time.
All of this promotes faith.

> Yet, with respect to the promise of God, he did not waver in
> unbelief, but grew strong in faith, giving glory to God, and
> being fully assured that what He had promised, He was able
> also to perform.

Romans 4:20–21

Many aspects of the believer's life have been made out to
be nearly impossible to accomplish. We are given reams of material on how to be a good parent, partner, and child of God.
There seems to be so much information that we must know.
How can we take it all in? How can we always do the right
thing? And those who present to us the much-needed information seem so much more spiritual than we are; they have
done the right things all along, and they even have degrees to
aid them in their success. However, Scripture does not indicate that being a parent, a mate, or a brother or sister in Christ
is all that difficult. In fact, there is very little in Scripture concerning what to do, but there are basic attitudes to hold.

> And so, as those who have been chosen of God, holy and
> beloved, put on a heart of compassion, kindness, humility, gen-
> tleness and patience; bearing with one another, and forgiving
> each other, whoever has a complaint against anyone; just as the
> Lord forgave you, so also should you.

Colossians 3:12–14

The Christian life is as simple as loving your wife, respect-
ing your husband, forgiving your enemy, not provoking your
children, obeying your parents, and working as though for the
Lord. This is your long-term plan. In keeping it day by day
you will see ups and downs, reversals, and what I like to call
the inevitable Christian hiccups, but never, never allow those

daily matters to sidetrack you from your long-term plan, which will reap its own reward in the fullness of time.

There is a story told of a man who gave seminars all over the world on what a Christian must do to be a success. The man died and went to heaven. The first day in heaven he decided to give one of his seminars. He scheduled the largest room, and thousands came to hear him. While he was speaking, he noticed that Jesus was seated in the front row taking one page of notes after another, and this puzzled the man. At the break the man ran to Jesus and asked why He, of all people, would be taking so many notes. Jesus replied, "You see, this is the first time I've heard any of this Myself!"

Doing makes the Christian life far too difficult! It is not the doing that must come first, but the believing. Doing, emphasizing immediate results, will not see you through to the end as will believing, which successfully carried along every person of faith in Scripture. God has given every believer in every conceivable situation absolute attitudes to be maintained. Continue to love, to submit, to train; you may not see directly the positive results of your attitude, but remember, this is your long-term plan, and in the midst of the ups and downs, your soul can remain calm.

Often in our quest for immediate relief we see in others (and they see in us) things to change. We set out to transform, either covertly or overtly, those around us; this is nothing less than control and playing God's role. If God believed another person's behavior was important to change, He would have already changed it! A change in the behavior of Job's friends would not have lessened his plight one bit. It was Job's trust in God and the long-term result of faith that kept him. The whole test was calculated to clean up Job, not to change others. Others actually played very little part in the scenario. God's role was primary, Job's secondary, and the role of others somewhere far behind.

6

Self-Indulgence

Passivity

Through years of passivity, many have come to believe that their wills and minds are something they cannot regulate. The enemy uses this subtle deception to convince Christians that there is no need to move forward, for they can no longer change the state in which they exist. They then come to believe that choosing is no longer within their control.

Take, for example, a man watching pornography on television and believing he is not free to get up and turn it off. He continues watching, all the while punishing himself and wondering why God doesn't change him. A woman who has tried to stop bullying her husband decides that she can't change. She thinks she has no choice, and her husband will have to accept her domineering manner. These examples show the work of the enemy on a passive will.

Often the reason that this deception can gain so much momentum is that the believer thinks his decision to change must be followed by doing something in his own strength. Because in his mind choosing and doing have essentially been combined into one action, and with memories of his inability to do in the past, he immediately gives in and refuses to even choose. Remember, though the choosing is our responsibility, the doing is always God's.

I once discipled a man who was addicted to pornography. He said that he simply could not choose to avoid stores peddling lascivious materials, for he had tried many times yet continued to frequent them. I explained that he could choose to have nothing more to do with pornography and allow God to be in charge of the doing. After all, if he possessed the strength for the doing, would he be sitting in my office in the first place? Together we prayed, and he expressed to God his desire to have nothing more to do with pornography; he made an active choice to let God do something for him. As he left the office he asked, "But what am I to do?"

I responded, "As you drive home tonight, do not concern yourself with the pornography, but continue to praise and thank God, who will deliver you by His action. Keep your eyes on the Doer and your choice to let Him take care of the problem." He called me later that evening and said that for the first time he drove by a store that sold pornographic materials and never wanted to stop, for he was too busy being grateful to God, our strong Deliverer. Granted, driving by only once was a small victory, and he would have to pass by many more times and be delivered as many times, but each deliverance would begin with the choice to allow God to be the Doer! "For it is God who is at work in you, both to will and to work for His good pleasure" (Phil. 2:13).

Many believers consider the characteristics of the apostle Paul and conclude that they could never have such a life. Why? Because they are accustomed to looking only at what they can do in their own strength. Some dress it up by saying they need God's help to live the Christian life, but the source of the doing remains themselves. Their eyes have yet to be opened to what God will do if they were to choose to let Him.

Many people have passive minds, the playgrounds of the enemy. No control is exercised over the thoughts that Satan freely places there. They have, no doubt, in the past attempted to reject thoughts of hatred, bitterness, anger, lust, and the like, but as the thoughts returned, they gave in to the notion that there must be a reason for them to be there. The truth that we can clean up our thought-life is evidenced by how hard the enemy fights to regain this ground when we begin to reject thoughts that do not fit the scriptural pattern of what is proper. "Finally, brethren, whatever is true, whatever is honorable, whatever is right, whatever is pure, whatever is lovely, whatever is of good repute, if there is any excellence and if anything worthy of praise, let your mind dwell on these things" (Phil. 4:8). One thing about the enemy we can learn during our journey in the narrow way is that he can be displaced easily, the proof being how hard he works through deception and fear to maintain his footing when we do something as simple as rejecting a thought.

A sister in Christ once approached me and stated that she was a terrible mother, because often while driving she would have thoughts about pushing her child out of the car. She had struggled and struggled with these thoughts and had concluded that she was definitely a very dangerous and insufficient mother. I explained to her that the very fact that she was wrestling with these notions proved that the ideas were not hers and in actuality were repulsive to her. Her contending revealed her true character: She was a good mother. The thoughts, however, did reveal the true nature of the devil, who would, if given the opportunity, push a helpless child out of a moving car. She had to regain the ground her passive mind let slip away by setting her mind on the God who with ease has overcome the enemy. She needed not to fight the thoughts, but to focus on the One who would cause the originator of the thoughts to flee. She was opposing the wrong thing by battling with thoughts and believing they were hers, instead of resisting the enemy who sent the thoughts. As she recognized his tactics and drew near to God, her mind was regained. "And do not be conformed to this world, but be transformed by the renewing of your mind, that you may prove what the will of God is, that which is good and acceptable and perfect" (Rom. 12:2).

As you continue your journey in the narrow way, make the choice to set your eyes on Jesus, rejecting the lying thoughts and emotions of the enemy. Remember, it is God who has called you to dwell daily in His presence.

Living in the Past

Far too many allow the enemy to continually draw their minds and emotions to events of the past, not only the distant past, but to occurrences of yesterday or the past hour. As we continue to dwell on the past, our movement in the Lord is immediately stopped, not to progress again until we regain the moment and the awareness of it. Satan—aware of all our failures, guilt, and fears—comes to us from our past and would have us live there, while God comes to us in the present with hope for the future. As believers we are to examine our ways for one reason: "Let us examine and probe our ways, And let us return to the LORD" (Lam. 3:40). It is quite sad to see believers who have their future in the Lord stolen by a continual examination of the past. Some even pay for counseling sessions that do the stealing.

Once we have allowed the problems, pressures, and events of this life to drive us into the narrow way that leads to God's presence, we are no longer bitter about those things, for we can trust God to use them. Why, then, should we continue to dwell on them? Part of our surrender to God is refusing to blame man for anything. The apostle Paul was told that he would die in Rome. He was delivered up by man to be put to death, but we do not find Paul blaming man for his condition. Instead, he receives it as coming from the very hand of God.

We must see everything that comes to us is by way of God. Once this is recognized, we will yield ourselves—including our reactions—to what God is doing.

Do you pout and cry when things have not gone your way? Or is there thankful joy in the midst of pain, which proclaims that God knows what He is doing? Our high calling does not include dwelling upon the past only to lose the moment in which God is at work.

Some time ago I visited with a couple seeking counsel about an upcoming court appearance concerning an injustice that had been done to them. They were not sure what they should say, since both of them knew how deceptive the person was with whom they had to appear. For the next several hours they related to me all the events that had brought them to such a predicament. Then I asked, "How long have you known about the upcoming hearing?"

They answered, "Approximately three months."

I then asked, "During that period, how many times have you discussed the details of this case with other believers?"

The response was, "Daily."

I explained that I was gravely concerned that they were in big trouble. The only way that they could have the words needed for such a situation was going daily before the Lord. For as we lay our hearts before Him, we find they are strengthened, encouraged, and filled; we gain the quiet confidence that all will go according to His will, whatever it might be. This couple had wasted those daily opportunities to be spiritually empowered by opting to discuss past events daily with man. They were now going to court with no inner preparation! Was it any wonder that they were undone and full of fear at the outcome? Nothing had come from their constant reiterating of the past except the loss of confidence in the future. And so it is with believers who continue to live in the past, neglecting the moment.

When I visit my family in Kansas, I always spend some time with my grandfather working on the farm. There always seems to be a lesson for me in what I observe. Andrew Murray once commented that all of creation preaches to us. That, of course, is why one evening of stargazing and contemplating our Creator can often do more for one's theology than three years of seminary. One time my job was to grade the feed lot, which had been recently used. Having had some experience around cattle, it was not difficult for me to spot each "cow patty"; I've stepped in them before and didn't enjoy it any more the last time than I did the first. The repeated encounters have taught me to watch where I step. I know all I care to know about manure!

Could you imagine my spending eight hours examining "cow patties" after all my unpleasant exposure to them? Would I know any more at the end of my inspection than experience had already taught me? Certainly not!

At this point you are justifiably wondering what all this has to do with the Christian life. Simply this: Many believers have had horrible experiences in earlier days, both before and after they accepted Christ. There is value in the initial understanding of how the ugly past makes them act, but only if that comprehension is coupled with realizing how the Lord chooses to free them from it once and for all. Too many continue to examine the past over and over and over again. The past is just that—past! What benefit can be derived from continual examination of something so smelly, rotten, and distasteful?

Why continue to dwell on how others have mistreated you, how your mate cheated on you, how your mother offended you, or how a believer used you? If you continue to live in the past, flipping it over, poking it with an intellectual stick, and examining it with an emotional eyeglass, you will learn no more than you already knew from your first understanding of it. You become a "cow-patty Christian," one who refuses to let go of the hurts, disappointments, and failures that came before and chooses to wallow in them. Instead of meditating on God in the present, you meditate on the past, which has become your focus, your god. At that point you are anything but the fra-

grant aroma that Paul commands believers to be. I promise
you that after I spent an afternoon in the feed lot with cow
patties, my wife wanted nothing to do with me. Similarly, very
few want to be with the "cow-patty Christian."

> But one thing I do: forgetting what lies behind and reaching
> forward to what lies ahead, I press on toward the goal for the
> prize of the upward call of God in Christ Jesus.
>
> Philippians 3:13–14

Bitterness: A Roadblock for the Married

WARNING!
DANGER AHEAD!
WATCH FOR FALLING DEBRIS!
NO ENTRY!
ONE WAY!

These are all road signs that we have learned to heed. They
convey warnings that, when observed, will protect life. If only
we had bright orange and yellow emotional warning signs that
would be taken as seriously!

For most things in life, it appears that there are primary
and secondary purposes. For example, the most important purpose of an automobile is to move people from point A to point
B; the lesser intent is to take them there comfortably. It would
be unfortunate if the priority of those objectives were turned
around. Then commuters and travelers could be at ease in lux-
urious interiors while they sit stranded by the roadside in cars
that have broken down.

Many have unfortunately reversed the primary and secondary objectives of marriage, making the secondary one—
happiness—preeminent. In actuality, the highest goal of marriage is to work Christ's life out of us, to squeeze us to reveal
the Christ within, to bring us out of self-centered existence

into Christ-centered living, and to reveal the joy of laying down our lives for another without being offended by walking in love and being willing to lose. When the primary purpose is fulfilled, the secondary purpose of happiness is inevitably experienced.

Anyone who believes that happiness is more than the by-product of marriage can reject his mate and look elsewhere for gratification. It is a deception, since enjoyment of the union is elusive until it is the result of learning the blessedness of laying down his life for someone he loves and who loves him. To continue to seek happiness without first completing God's primary purpose in marriage is not only extremely selfish but is like purchasing an auto without a good engine. No matter how attractive it looks, it will go nowhere!

If I had a dollar for each time I have heard the following complaints, I could live quite comfortably. They come from a husband or wife whom Satan has blinded to all the warning signs; it is a story of destruction, deep defeat, and deception. The outpouring is cross-cultural; I have heard it in over thirty countries. It is a good example of the roadblock of bitterness, which develops very slowly from the germinal stages of a relationship and, if not recognized and denied, hinders the presence of God. This particular roadblock can yield the following: "My mate is not meeting my needs. [Needs that a mate never could meet, for they can only be satisfied by God.] If I continue to stay with him (or her), I will suffocate. Soon my whole life will have vanished before my very eyes. I must get out now while there is still time for happiness. There is nothing I can do to please my mate. He will never change, and why should I change for him?"

Once these thoughts have firmly rooted themselves in the believer's heart, an emotional divorce, which always precedes intellectual and physical divorce, will take place. A person goes through considerable conflict before undergoing emotional divorce, and I have found that seldom will he return to his mate once this has occurred. To arrive at the point of divorce, one must weigh and struggle with all the consequences that will be the result of this decision—the children, friends, family, the respect of others, position in the church and society, and even one's own self-respect and morals—until somehow the variables are jockeyed into the position where one comes out the apparent winner. The vindicated victim pictures himself or herself as some kind of self-fashioned martyred saint for giving so much for so long and having received so little. He or she now deserves, in return, a life free from the ugly tyrant who has caused such misery. Don't try to point out the flaws in this person's logic, for to him the issue is ironed out and makes perfect sense. All he needs is a counselor to agree with the decision and to praise him for his years of sacrifice and for the bold step he has now taken to save himself.

The mate on the receiving end of an emotional divorce is going to be rejected and confused by this behavior. Life for him or her will become quite intolerable, for in order for the emotionally divorcing spouse to continue pressing on toward physical divorce, the decision must be intellectually justified. The mate is targeted; every offense he has ever committed will be called to his attention. On a scale of one to ten, every shortcoming he's displayed in the past will become a ten. Attempts will be made to make him angry, violent, withdrawn, or irrational in order for the aggressor to be able to proclaim to the world (after having pushed the mate to such behavior) that this is evidence of the wisdom of the decision to move out of the relationship.

At this point the individual pursuing divorce is darkened in his conscience; he dances with the devil, walks without light, and even allows Satan to use scriptural premises to prod him. "God's love is unconditional, and even if it is sin to divorce, every sin is forgivable. What makes it worse than any other sin?" "David committed adultery, and look at how God used him." "It may cost me something, but the kids will get over it. After all, they should know that we live in a world where people do get divorced." Concurrently, the enemy points to all the narrow-minded, hypocritical Christians who will treat him differently, who will not hold his hand through this period of suffering, and who must all be blind to the fact that *he* was the one who *really* suffered all those years.

By this juncture it is as though Satan gains a devotee, one who will do his bidding, who is blind to consequence, and who has eaten anew from the tree of the knowledge of good and evil and now must know more than God. The root of bitterness is firmly entrenched in the hardened heart. What can be said or done for such a one? He has exalted himself to the position of knowing what is best, though it opposes God's words. So persuaded is he that his mate has oppressed him and made his life miserable that he actually will sense a false release when he does legally divorce.

During Christ's ministry on earth, there was approximately an eighteen-month period in which he was well liked. The Pharisees and the Sadducees were beginning to wonder if this Jesus might become the next king; He definitely had the following of the people, and even some of the Romans were listening to Him. The Pharisees approached Jesus and asked one question, which we can assume was uppermost among their concerns about what they could retain if Jesus came to power. The request sounded very much like this: "Moses allowed us to divorce. Will you?" The response from Jesus was immediate and cutting. "Because of your hardness of heart, Moses permitted you to divorce your wives; but from the beginning it has not been this way" (Matt. 19:7–8).

Emotional divorce does not reveal the shortcomings of the mate who is being left; rather, it reveals the hardness of the heart within the one who is leaving. We must remember there are only two types of people who have anything to do with sheep: butchers and shepherds. The butcher's voice is harsh, critical, driving, self-justifying, condemning of others, fault-finding, and immoral. Our Shepherd's voice does not keep a record of wrongs, encourages, gives life, brings light to our path, and grants the grace to receive the insults of others (Col.

3:12–14). To which voice have the emotionally divorcing been listening?

It is disturbing that many within the body of Christ have resigned themselves to the reality of divorce among God's people. There are many church seminars that help those who have divorced, but wouldn't it be wonderful if God's people never reached the place where a divorce was unavoidable? I'm not saying that there is no biblical justification for divorce, and many are quick to give a defense for those who fall into this category; I do that, also. However, the majority of divorces that I observe have the above-mentioned cause: *the sin of self-centeredness*. This sin causes deep destruction in Christian homes and in the children who are knocked down in its wake.

If you are in the process of creating an emotional divorce, what are you to do? First, get scared! You do not know the severity of that with which you play. Second, take some time away, even if it's just a day or two. During that period do not think about the situation, your mate, or your children; only look to Jesus. Take a simple passage (such as Psalm 139) and read it through, meditating on the Lord. Make Him your focus! Dwell on nothing else. During this time you will enter into divine sanity. How will you recognize divine sanity? It will make sense to you to forgive, to persevere, to be offended, and to be used. Losing your life in order that others might live will become more appealing. In a word, you will become obedient. The enemy would have you believe that once all issues are resolved, you can return to God; however, the truth is that returning to God resolves all issues. You may say, "I've tried to let God do it," and in that statement you reveal the depth of your deception. No one has to *try* to let God do anything. Give it; He will take it. What you are actually saying is that God has not resolved it in the way you think He ought to or according to your time schedule. Third, you must repent and, through that, reclaim the ground lost to the enemy. Give up the emotional and physical affairs with those other than your mate and let God do the forgiving and cleansing.

If you are the mate of one who is emotionally divorcing you, what are you to do? Pray, pray, and pray some more, for your battle is not against flesh and blood but against principalities and powers. It will do you no good to appeal to logic, to work harder, to cry, beg, plead, or to run to others for support, for the emotionally divorcing spouse has made his choice, and the only decision he wants to receive from you is one that agrees with his. So pray, knowing that unless God opens your mate's eyes to see the true source of his deception, he is lost to you. Be on guard, since the emotionally divorcing person wants to prove the very worst of you so he can appear to be the very best.

How does a godly person act on hearing that his mate has actually decided to leave him? Even the most devout would probably be full of fear, worry, anxiety, doubt, and depression, and would probably spend a fair amount of time weeping. How can we know such things? First Corinthians 7:15! Paul had noticed such behaviors and feelings, and so advises that if the unbelieving mate (his use of unbelief does not merely mean a person who is not going to heaven, but rather one who rejects the path of God) desires to depart, the believing mate is not bound, for God has called that person to peace (the opposite of the above-mentioned distress). Paul obviously had seen the opposite of peace in the distraught believers and knew that God had called them to something quite different. Agitation is normal for a Christian whose marriage is ending.

The mate being left should pray about how to react, for many times the unbelieving mate is petitioned to return, a change of emotions or guilt takes place, and he returns, only to leave at a later time. It is a common mistake to confuse a change in the emotions for a change of heart. When this occurs, the believing mate will simply have to suffer all over again as the unbeliever goes away in time.

Having completed several thousand hours of counseling, I can say with all confidence that divorce is disheartening and damaging, disclosing hard hearts.

It is valuable to understand biblical oneness. Oneness in marriage is often depicted as a circle with a line drawn through the middle. One half represents the man and the other, the woman; the two halves equal two individuals attempting to learn how to live as one. This same illustration is also used when describing the Father and Son, Christ in our spirits, and our relationship to one another in the body of Christ.

Biblical oneness, however, is really quite different. Imagine placing in a bowl both milk and flour. They are not one until they are blended together, and after that they cannot be separated. If food coloring is added during the blending process, the hue of the whole mixture is changed.

When a man and woman marry, they are not two individuals attempting to live as one. God puts the man and woman in the bowl, turns on His divine mixer, and the two become one. Since the divine mixer is always running, if one mate throws dirt at the other, it irrefutably dirties his whole being as well. Many need to lose their individuality (not personality) and come to understand that they are one with their mates, the Lord Jesus, and the body of Christ. Once the reality of oneness is revealed, we do the most we can for the upbuilding of our mates, we see clearly that what is true of Christ is true of us, and we refuse to cause damage to the body of Christ. What God has joined together, let no one separate (John 10:30; 14:9; 17:11–12; John 15; 1 Cor. 6:17; 12:12).

Father, deliver your people from this monster named divorce; deliver us from unbelief, the mother of all sin, and teach us Your ways! "'For I hate divorce,' says the LORD, the God of Israel" (Mal. 2:16).

Taking God's Job

Many believers are unable to distinguish between their job as sheep and the job of the Shepherd. Therefore, many take on themselves the responsibility that is God's alone. When I encounter such a believer, I often show him a picture of a shepherd and his sheep and ask such questions as "Whose job is it to discern the will of the shepherd; is it not his job to reveal it?" "Whose job is it to make sure that the sheep remain on the correct path and to seek them out when they are lost?" "Whose job is it to find food and refreshment for the sheep and to protect the sheep from all evil?" "Would a shepherd send another sheep to seek out the lost lamb?"

We are the creatures and He is the magnificent Creator. The Christian life is not a life that is difficult to live when the true responsibilities of the Shepherd are revealed. It is a life that can be lived by even the weakest believer.

Once a believer shared with me about a seminar she had attended on how to pray. The program included instruction on how to meditate until the face of the Lord could be seen and His voice heard. Very few attending the conference were able to attain such an experience. My response was that such teaching was without question from the enemy. The sister asked me how I could be so confident, and I responded that any teaching that I could not carry out must be false. Her response was quite logical: "Who do you think you are?"

"I'm the simplest believer I know, and if I cannot move into the presence of God through some teaching, then that teaching is wrong." I explained that the deep Christian truths are for even the weakest of believers and that she had already been hearing God's voice.

As mentioned previously, there are two forms of discipleship in the church today. The predominant form emphasizes what may one day be possessed through hard work, and it manipulates the disciple through guilt by constantly comparing him with others who have arrived. The approach less often utilized teaches what a believer already possesses, stressing those things that can be experienced through God's work today and inspiring action through the understanding of the love and compassion of God. It is unfortunate that the former agenda reigns in Christendom today.

It is worthwhile to examine the differences between these approaches to discipleship. In the former, success is determined by grand accomplishments: numbers, individual decisions, buildings, giving, programs, attendance, passages memorized, rules kept, levels of separation, submission gained, and devotion to structure. Exaltation, superiority, and authority are the buzzwords, rather than equality. Discipleship takes the form of a mold that can make parrots of those deemed superior in discipline, while God's loving hand in the lives of the weak, defeated, and failing is never considered. The desire to wait on God while receiving nothing, the giving of a kind word when slandered or misunderstood, and the ability to love the unlovable are not considered cherished traits. A full notebook and head full of knowledge are preferred to a heart that is full to overflowing. The knowledge of the Bible takes precedence over knowledge of the Author. Law of and for the earth is more valuable than grace that originates in heaven. Disciples are equipped only to see the steps needed to secure God but remain ignorant of God's work to secure them. They are continually taught how to change, yet remain untutored regarding the secret of expanding the life, *His* life, which is already possessed. These disciples are in the bondage of comparison, never enjoying their youth in the Lord. Soul and spirit are not divided, leading them to believe that great talent, intellect, and ability will equal both great spiritual power and pleasure to God. Slow, steady, and natural growth is abandoned for the promised one-time fix. The leader sets the standard for success in the participants' walks with God, using his own experiences and attainments as the standard rather than God's standard, which allows for *individualized* success. Many are the victims of legalistic discipleship.

When someone states that he cannot hear God, the teachers from the first school immediately confide how they hear God and encourage the believer to imitate them. When the teachers from the second school hear such a statement, they immediately impart the confidence that it is impossible for the struggling believer not to hear God, for His sheep hear His voice. It is God's job to sort out and define the voice of the Shepherd that the believer has been hearing all along.

In true discipleship we are to reveal to the elect all that they already possess as members of the flock of the Shepherd. Christianity is simple!

Disobedience

Obedience can be a roadblock in the Christian's walk simply because its unique qualities lend themselves to misunderstanding. The fear of obedience can hinder a believer's walk for a long time. Obedience is without question the most delicate and dangerous topic in the Christian life for two reasons.

First, there are those who avoid the topic altogether. They overlook the fact that obedience is predominant from the beginning of Genesis, where obedience is the one requirement of inhabiting the garden, to the last chapter of the Revelation, where obedience allows the believer to eat from the tree of life.

Second, when it is taught, obedience is actually much more dangerous than when it is avoided, for the wrong instruction on obedience will actually encourage sin. This is the problem that Paul had in discussing obedience. The flesh-life of man is all too willing to look for something that calls for self-effort and casts away the grace of God. Read some of what Paul tells the believers in Galatians, chapters 4 and 5.

> But now that you have come to know God, or rather to be known by God, how is it that you turn back to the weak and worthless elemental things, to which you desire to be enslaved all over again?
>
> Galatians 4:9

> Where then is that sense of blessing you had?
>
> Galatians 4:15

You have been severed from Christ, you who are seeking to be justified by law; you have fallen from grace.

Galatians 5:4

For you were called to freedom, brethren.

Galatians 5:13

Obedience is one of the easiest topics to be mistaught simply because man has keen awareness of his own failure. We have had failure pointed out to us repeatedly, and we have been manipulated by that failure at the hands of others. Therefore, it is quite simple for obedience to take on the very ugly and demonic twist of being equal to and necessary for acceptance.

"Obedience equals acceptance" is actually the proper definition of legalism, which teaches that by obeying we can be more acceptable to God. Legalism will, in turn, drive a believer away from God and into self-effort. If obedience did equal acceptance, Jesus would never have had to come to earth. As it is, our favorable reception by God is based on Christ's behavior, not ours. We could not be acceptable to God when we were outside of Christ no matter how good our behavior was, and now that we are in Christ, we will not be made unacceptable no matter how bad our actions become. That is not to say that the believer who does not carry out the commands will not be disciplined, but this correction comes because he is a child of God, not in order that he might become a child of God. How easy it is to forget that obedience is not the cause of our relationship with Christ, but the result of it.

The problem is that when we are told that obedience will equal acceptance, we immediately avoid it at all cost! Why? Because in the past we tried to become acceptable through our behavior and were unsuccessful; therefore, we feel that our present effort can only be one more failure in the making. We may now find ourselves running from obedience, not wanting the pain of falling short again.

When we believe that obedience equals acceptance, even the Scriptures that were to be a means of blessing to us become a source of discouragement. For the legalist reads the Scriptures as though through a pair of glasses that distort all that is read, and so he sees only what must be done to be acceptable. Legalism is rampant in the church. On one occasion when I had the privilege of speaking to several hundred believers, I asked the question "What are five things you must do to assure and maintain your growth, holiness, family life, and faith?" Immediately I received the following answers: prayer, the Word, fellowship, discipline, and quiet times. Next, I asked the question "What are five things God is doing to assure and maintain your growth, holiness, family life, and faith?" The audience was silent! We easily understand what we are to do, but all too often are ignorant when it comes to understanding what God is doing.

Andrew Murray once commented that the worst heresy in the church was the continual emphasis on what we must do, without understanding what God is doing for us. Christianity is not to be viewed as a man-based religion, the paramount significance of which is what we do, but is a relationship with God that rests in His work and "the strength of His might." If success is based on man, then we obviously are neglecting "the surpassing greatness of His power toward us who believe"(Eph. 1:19).

Grasping the knowledge of all scriptural commands will not secure the presence of God, which is something that is given to us as the basis for the outgrowth of our spiritual lives, not something that we can earn through self-effort and obedience. The path to abundant life is narrow, yes, but not the tightrope—which few can walk—that legalism professes it to be.

Obedience does not equal acceptance! If we believe that it does, then we are doomed to failure and certain frustration, for God will do nothing to encourage that false theology. We are acceptable because Christ's life, the only acceptable life to God, dwells within us to become our very life. Any discussion concerning obedience must first establish that acceptance is based in Christ rather than in obedience. If a believer is never obedient, he will still be acceptable in Christ. Was it obedience that brought you into a relationship with God, or was it a new birth through faith? Likewise, is it possible for disobedience to take you out of your relationship with God?

What, then, is the purpose of obedience? Let me answer by way of analogy. Have you ever had an appetite for something but were not sure just what it was? When this happens, don't you normally go through the kitchen cupboards looking for that one item to eat that will satisfy the desire? As you sample a few items, tasting and looking for the perfect food to relieve the craving, you slowly become full, but not really satisfied. Finally you spot the chocolate chips and immediately realize that this is what you wanted all along. You stop after eating just a few, gratified.

We are all born as unbelievers with Adam's life within, a life with a craving for disobedience. The unregenerate may eat of several things, but will not be satisfied except with their fill of misdeeds.

There are in the world many unfulfilled unbelievers who have not yet had the opportunity to partake of all desired iniquities. This is why unregenerate man busies himself with reversing all the laws and harsh punishments that hinder his disobedience.

On the other hand, when a person is born again, he receives a new, righteous life—Christ's life—which hungers for obedience. Christ's life within a believer longs for obedience as the only thing that will satisfy! The question for a Christian is not whether to be acceptable or unacceptable, a sinner or righteous, spiritual or carnal, a success or a failure; the choice is whether to be satisfied or unsatisfied. A believer yearns for obedience as the sole means of filling up the craving within. When it comes to the preference of disobedience versus obedience, it is merely a choice between eating dog food or steak and lobster. Dog food will not satisfy; steak and lobster will!

And the contrast between the two is so great that it is really no challenge at all to choose obedience. Paul does not continually portray the Christian life as one of struggling between obedience and disobedience; rather, he assumes that obedience is something that we not only want but have the power to grasp.

Do you want to be full? Then obey! For obedience is what you are craving.

One brother told me that he felt empty, experiencing a deep longing within and a dissatisfaction with life. He had concluded that the source of his problem was his wife and that he should leave her for another woman who, in theory, would cure the hunger pangs within. My response was, "Brother, the yearning you have described is no less than a craving for obedience. If you would savor life, then obey by loving the wife you have."

Once we comprehend that the purpose of obedience is to make us full and that we do not have the added pressure of performing for acceptance, obedience becomes quite simple.

How much effort is involved in eating our favorite foods? Do we count it a chore, an insurmountable task, or even a struggle to purchase the cakes or ice cream so cherished? Do we find it a burden to pay for the foods that we crave? No, we never count the cost, for there is too much satisfaction in such things.

Once we see obedience as the true food for which we long, in every situation we will begin to ask ourselves, "Do I want to be full or not? Do I want to be satisfied?" We will actually begin to look for opportunities to be obedient. If we enter a room in which others are slandering us, and we comply by loving our enemies, we can leave the room full, satisfied, and with a lift in our spirits. If we forgive, lay down our lives for our brothers, train our eyes and tongues, if we bring every thought captive to Christ, and give as He has given to us, we will be no closer to God or more acceptable, but we will be full. We will be satisfied.

I now understand why David so loved the commands of God. Once I could see the purpose in keeping them, I, too, have come to love the commands, to love obedience, for I love to be satisfied and full to overflowing.

Once at a retreat in the mountains attended by several Christian men from different countries, we decided to try our hand at panning for gold. One of the brothers asked if it was a wise use of time to continue looking for gold when there were more pressing spiritual matters to which to attend. Just as he was speaking, one of the other men found what at the time appeared to be gold, and we all started unearthing it frantically. As I dug, I turned to my right, where to my amazement I saw the brother who thought we ought to be doing something more spiritual shoveling with us. I commented that I was confused about his activity, since it was of no spiritual value, and without looking at me he said, "I didn't know until this moment how much I really liked gold!" Until he actually saw it, he was not stirred. I can say the same thing about obedience; it wasn't until I saw its purpose that I found out how much I really liked it.

If obedience is the quenching nourishment for the life within, do not these words of Jesus compel us to be obedient in every situation?

> In the meanwhile the disciples were requesting Him, saying, "Rabbi, eat." But He said to them, "I have food to eat that you do not know about." The disciples therefore were saying to one another, "No one brought Him anything to eat, did he?" Jesus said to them, "My food is to do the will of Him who sent Me, and to accomplish His work."
>
> John 4:31–34

The Jesus who stated what His true food was is the very same Jesus with the very same appetite that lives within you. You know what to feed His life, so you can always find the joy of being satisfied.

Obsession with Sin

When it comes to the topic of battling sin, there is one rule that must never be broken: When we battle sin, we are never to battle sin! No, we are never to fight sin if we desire to overcome it.

Let me illustrate. There is a story of a fellow in India who was traveling from village to village selling a magic potion. The man would ask for a clean bucket, into which he poured clear water and some of the magic potion. As he stirred the mixture, through sleight of hand he would drop in three or four nuggets of gold. When the water was drained off, there was the gold. In one community, a money changer was watching the demonstration and asked if he could purchase the formula for fifty thousand rupees. The fellow was more than happy to sell, and after receiving the payment, he turned to the money changer and said, "There is one thing you must never do while making the gold, or else the potion will not work. While stirring the water and adding the formula, you must never, never think of the red-faced monkey!" As you can well imagine, the money changer was never able to make gold! Wherever he went, from the Himalayas to the south of India, no matter how hard he worked to block it, the red-faced monkey would pop into his mind.

So it is with sin. Unless you shift your focus away from it, you will never overcome it. I have often commented that God has delivered me from many things, but not once was I freed from anything on which I was centered.

Many have focused on their sin ten, twenty, thirty, and even forty years, and it has become so much a part of their lives that they are not even sure what they would do if they were to be miraculously delivered. If 25 percent of thought-life is concentrated on something that is consuming, and immediate deliverance were to occur, exactly what would replace that portion of mental energy? What would fill the vacuum?

The solution to warring against sin is setting our minds on something other than the sin. This cannot be done by consciously avoiding the sin, but rather by resolutely making the Lord the focus of daily thought-life. "Do not be conformed to this world, but be transformed by the renewing of your mind, that you may prove what the will of God is, that which is good and acceptable and perfect" (Rom. 12:2). If our focus is kept on things worldly rather than on that which pertains to the kingdom of God, we will be led to Christian fatalism, the belief that this life in the body will constantly be given up to defeat and misery. Thus we will accept continual suffering as the norm and merely wait until the time when we are caught up into the relief of the rich experience that is heaven. The truth is that all suffering has its purpose of producing joyful, abundant living in the presence of God right now.

Part 3

Life
in His Presence

7

Enjoyment
of His Presence

As believers, after passing through the series of roadblocks on the way to God's presence, we discover something quite wonderful and beautiful. We have always possessed God's presence; it was something we sought after but already owned. "Where can I go from Thy Spirit? Or where can I flee from Thy presence?" (Ps. 139:7). We did not recognize and utilize the presence of God because we were content to trust ourselves to govern the misfortunes of daily life. It took a unique set of problems, circumstances, and sins to make us realize we were not equipped to overcome apart from the Vine. We also needed to discover the victory that was ours in Christ as we overcame each roadblock. This triumph was given to us, not earned. This information becomes invaluable as we lead others into God's presence.

As we now stand in the realization that we are in God's presence, the very place the Savior intended to bring us long ago, where every complaint of spirit, soul, and body is laid to rest, we break out in praise.

But God, being rich in mercy, because of His great love with
which He loved us, even when we were dead in our transgres-
sions, made us alive together with Christ (by grace you have
been saved), and raised us up with Him, and seated us with
Him in the heavenly places, in Christ Jesus, in order that in the
ages to come He might show the surpassing riches of His grace
in kindness toward us in Christ Jesus.

Ephesians 2:4–7

In His presence we find the greatest joy and, in turn, are
a joy to the Lord. We are now willing to enter into the holy
place by the blood of Jesus with *confidence*, knowing all requests will be heard, not on the basis of behavior, but because
of the Son's demeanor and stature. With this awareness, the
disciples' requests begin to change; no longer do we want for
ourselves the petty things of life, for we are confident our needs
will be met. Instead we ask for what might glorify the Son, for
people to be given to the Son in order that the Son might present them to the Father. In God's light, we can put together
the missing pieces of the Christian life. The commands are
viewed as promises, present suffering is not to be compared
with God's glory, and divine sanity becomes a way of life. It
makes sense to obey, for in His presence there is power with
the command; it is logical to press on, for in His presence there
is assurance that He will take us on! It is reasonable to forgive,
for in His presence His forgiveness is overwhelming. Waiting
is not a forced activity, for there is complete confidence that
the promise is worth as much as its fulfillment.

The psalmists found divine sanity in the presence of God.
"When I pondered to understand this, it was troublesome in
my sight until I came into the sanctuary of God; then I perceived their end" (Ps. 73:16–17). For David it was wise to love,
for in God's presence there is love to spare.

Faith is no strain when we gaze at the mystery of His working and know that there is nothing He cannot accomplish. Suffering need no longer be met by dismay when accompanied by

the knowledge that there is no pain that His presence does not overcome in such a way that we are made more than conquerors.

There is indeed nothing that His presence does not cure. We have found it, we cannot lose it, and no one can take it from us.

> For I am convinced that neither death, nor life, nor angels, nor principalities, nor things present, nor things to come, nor powers, nor height, nor depth, nor any other created thing, shall be able to separate us from the love of God, which is in Christ Jesus our Lord.
>
> Romans 8:38–39

If His presence is too absent from our Christian lives, we are stripped of the joy we ought to have in our work. Is this not why Bible reading, prayer, witnessing, church attendance, and spiritual battles are void of the anticipation that Jesus demonstrated throughout His life? His presence must become our nourishment for the tasks at hand, for He is the true bread to be eaten.

There is one major danger once we are enjoying His presence. We must realize that attempting to secure His presence will only cause its loss, for it is not given to reward effort but rather through faith. As we learn to abide in it day by day and moment by moment, we will begin to experience how unchangeable is life in the Spirit. The awareness of our uninterrupted fellowship in the Spirit will have a calming effect on the mind, will, and emotions, which in turn will still the body, allowing us to live in a hostile world, possessing His peace.

The Presence Within

Where is the kingdom of God? Where are we to look for it? The Pharisees had the same questions, and the answer that Jesus gave them is appropriate for us as well. "The kingdom of God is not coming with signs to be observed; nor will they say, 'Look, here it is!' or, 'There it is!' For behold, the kingdom of God is within you" (Luke 17:20–21 NIV). Many have looked in a church, to a vocation, or at this place or that person, but we must never look for the kingdom anywhere other than within, where Christ dwells. "Christ lives in me" (Gal. 2:20). "Christ in you, the hope of glory" (Col. 1:27). "Christ is formed in you" (Gal. 4:19). "So that Christ may dwell in your hearts through faith" (Eph. 3:17). "Sanctify Christ as Lord in your hearts" (1 Peter 3:15).

The point being made is this: If we would dwell in the presence of God moment by moment, then we look to the Christ within to find His abiding presence. Saint Augustine once said that he had lost much time in the beginning of his Christian experience by trying to find the Lord outwardly rather than by turning inward.

There is great benefit in recognizing that the kingdom of God is within. In the Lord's Prayer we ask that His kingdom come and His will be done on earth as it is in heaven. The expression of the heavenly must come into our hearts before it can be manifested to those on the earth. As we look to the Christ within, His life is released in us, displaying to those around us the very substance of His kingdom. The beauty of this exhibition is as natural as a flower on a fruit tree; it is not contrived, but is a fragrant aroma to all who can discern and receive it.

As we look within, Jesus will teach us daily, leaving a lasting imprint on our hearts. This is the kind of teaching we long for, that which is delivered with power.

For so many years I studied the Scriptures in order to one day be an apt teacher. Reading commentaries, studying Greek, and outlining passage after passage, I prepared to impart the proper knowledge. I discovered after much academic study that this kind of examination would not put me in contact with the living God. My mistake was to believe that if I, as well as others, possessed the proper knowledge, we would do what was right and honorable. "You search the Scriptures, because you think that in them you have eternal life; and it is these that bear witness of Me" (John 5:39). I stopped seeking to know about God and began to wonder how I could know God.

Imagine that instead of your having a wife or a husband, I were to merely give you pictures and letters from a spouse. Would that suffice? Whenever you were longing for a mate, my response would be, "Get out the letters and pictures," or, "Maybe you should write a letter yourself." Would this kind of pen-pal relationship be fulfilling?

Neither is God interested in a pen-pal who reads His letters, looks at His pictures, and sends Him worrisome messages once in awhile. He wants you to come in contact with Him. He has made it unbelievably simple by placing His very life within you. If you were only quiet for a moment, you could hear His voice teaching you with power to change your heart.

Why is it that so many possess so much knowledge and yet so little power? Is it not because their knowledge did not come from a Christ within, but rather Scripture without? Once I learned this secret, I was surprised to find that by looking to Christ within, I could receive, often in less than one minute, a message to teach. To my further amazement, when a communication of this type was then developed and delivered, it went forth with power and was life changing to the hearers. These messages that were received in so short a time from Him had more spiritual power in one sentence than a whole sermon developed out of my own resources and research.

One of my beloved mentors in the faith in India tells of a time when he wanted more than anything else to see the face of Jesus. He felt that if only the Lord were to appear to him, he would have the needed confidence for the task ahead. So he determined to fast and pray to elicit the Lord's revelation of Himself. Well into the night of the fourth day, he was alerted by a knock at the door. He sensed in his spirit that he would actually see Jesus. Upon opening the door, he discovered a half-naked, malnourished, and unattractive young man, and he noticed that flies were swarming around the dirty youth, who offered this explanation. "Do you want to know why these flies swarm around me? They swarm around me because I am dung. My mother and father have rejected me, and all others despise me. I am dung!" At that the young man turned and walked away.

When the door closed, my teacher heard the Lord speak. "Now you have seen My face! Where there is suffering, where there is pain, where there is rejection, there am I!" My teacher had prayed, he had sought the Christ within, and the teaching came with a power that left a permanent imprint on his heart. This man now radiates the love of Christ toward the downtrodden in a way that is rarely seen. He visits the leprosy hospitals, holds the untouchables, and gives Christ's love without measure. My mother, upon meeting this man, described him as an "Indian angel."

So it is for those who find Christ within; there is no lack of power, no sense of broken fellowship, only the continuous flow of His life. "Do you not know that you are a temple of God, and that the Spirit of God dwells in you?"(1 Cor. 3:16).

There is another advantage to discovering the Christ within: Silence becomes a blessing. While we are busy looking for Christ here and there and feeling that we cannot find Him, we long for the assurance of His voice. His speaking to us could calm our search and assure us that we had found Him, or at least that He has not abandoned us. But once we find through faith the Christ within, silence no longer bothers us; in fact, it becomes quite enjoyable. So few know the blessings that silence produces, for the majority are too busy giving God the orders for the day, clamoring to make sure He both hears them and acts in a way that will serve their best interests. They miss the awareness of His presence revealed in silence. Silence is important to God; it is mentioned over one hundred times in the Bible.

I enjoy my wife in various relationships—the spiritual, the physical, the emotional, and the sexual. We relate to each other in different ways at different times. The one relationship not mentioned, which took the longest time to develop, was that of silence. There are many times when my wife and I are together that I want no discussion. When I am reading, there is silence, but I like knowing that she is there with me at the other end of the sofa. It is a very warm awareness and calmness that I experience. I simply want to abide in her presence as she does in mine. What makes this silence so satisfying is that I know that she wants to be there with me, and she knows I desire to be with her. Neither of us are requiring much from the other, but we are merely enjoying each other's presence. Being there near me is all I ask of her during those silent times, for I love her. When all the doing is stripped away, we are really content just to have each other's presence.

We the church are the bride of Christ. Are we content with Him alone, or do we only desire Him when He gives something we want? Can we be content with the warmth of His presence in silence, or must we continually be talking, arguing, and soliciting? If we received nothing more from His hand the rest of our lives other than the awareness of this Christ within, and if He were to remain silent, would we be filled to overflowing?

Many have never taken the time to be silent before the Lord. Many do not know how. I can say with assurance that they have suffered a great loss in all their talking, searching, and commanding. If we seek Him for our own enjoyment, to receive emotional, physical, and spiritual needs, we err, since we should seek Him for His enjoyment. All who have sought God for His enjoyment will testify that they have been filled to overflowing, never disappointed by a single minute spent in His presence. Stop requesting all the frills from God; love Him in silence, learn to enjoy His presence within, and out of your innermost being will flow rivers of living water.

How do we begin to experience this blessed life of the presence within? By asking the One who has called us into such a deep personal relationship to reveal it to us. As we remain silent and dependent, He will remain faithful to complete that to which He has called us.

I have found that intellectual doctrine is much easier to communicate than spiritual truths, which are mysteries not fully understood but intended to be fully experienced. I have watched and even assisted in my wife's giving birth to three children. I have studied the process thoroughly. She has even explained to me in detail what she experienced in delivery. I have held each newborn minutes after birth. Yet to this day I cannot fathom what it is like to give birth to an infant. My wife has no trouble relating the experience to other mothers, and I watch as they simply give an insightful nod to the details. However, I know I will never fully understand.

So it is with spiritual truth. Those who have experienced Christ within may do a very poor job of explaining it, yet other believers with similar experience need only give a knowing nod. Spiritual realities, like birth, are miracles that come from the hand of God. And He is a God of miracles!

8

Prayer
in His Presence

What Is Prayer?

What exactly is prayer? Much has been written about the
subject, and books are plentiful on how we are to pray, for
what, and from where. However, I would like to discuss a forgotten aspect of prayer, which is listening. As we grow quiet
and draw near to the Christ within, we can begin to listen to
His voice and be refreshed and encouraged.

First of all, it will be important that we clarify just what it
is for which we are listening. Jesus' voice, He stated unequiv-
ocally, is simply and fully discernable. "My sheep hear My voice,
and I know them, and they follow Me" (John 10:27). This is
an absolute statement by Jesus. His voice must be clearly dis-
tinguishable. Yet many seem unable to hear His voice; they are
constantly confused by the voices around them, not certain if
they are hearing Satan, God, conscience, or their own fluctu-
ating emotions.

How can it be, then, that Jesus says His voice is readily heard? For the answer to that question, we must observe Christ's teaching in John 8, prior to His statement above. First He states, "I am the light of the world; he who follows Me shall not walk in the darkness, but shall have the light of life" (v. 12). Then he makes a second point: "If you abide in My word, then you are truly disciples of Mine; and you shall know the truth, and the truth shall make you free" (vv. 31–32). If we follow Him, He will guide us into the light, and as we abide in His Word, we will hear Him, know the truth, and be set free.

Jesus then gives a parable about a good shepherd to emphasize His previous teaching. There would not have been a person in His audience who did not understand the parable, for all were accustomed to the habits of shepherds and sheep. It was the shepherd's responsibility to guide the sheep to the place where they would be safe and receive nourishment. It is the responsibility of the Son of man to lead His followers out of darkness into light. It was also the responsibility of the shepherd to teach the sheep to hear his voice. If a shepherd had a sheep that never learned his voice as a lamb, he would use his staff to break its leg. The leg would be bandaged, and the sheep would have to be carried on the shoulders of the shepherd and hand fed until healed. During this time of weakness, the sheep would abide in the words of the shepherd and learn to hear his voice.

Similarly, a newborn baby, in its weakness, can do nothing to provide for himself and does the only thing a newborn can—abide in the mother's presence, learning her voice. In time, the voice and touch of the mother become quite unmistakable, even to the point at which the child will allow no one else to comfort or hold him. He knows his mother's voice with certainty.

Why then is it that so few believers seem to know the voice of the Lord Jesus? Is it not because they were never given the opportunity to learn His voice when they were babes in Christ and should have been discovering it? At that time learning the voice would have been natural, for there would have been nothing else they could have done in their infant state. Unfortunately, the church suffers from the avoidance of the basics. New converts who possess a measure of talent, ability, and intellect are all too often immediately put to work. No abilities must go unnoticed; they must be used, used, and used again. If they are not, then the cry is, "What a waste," just as the disciple deplored Mary's breaking the costly perfume at Jesus' feet and "wasting" what could have been used. When we neglect the basics, we unknowingly opt for more drastic measures that must be taken at a later time. Those who have not learned the Master's voice in infancy will often have to undergo the more extreme methods of breaking. They are immobilized for a protractive period in order to discover what should have been ascertained years before.

Why, then, do many not know His voice? They have never taken or been given the opportunity to lay before the Lord in silence, abiding in His words and thus being able to distinguish His voice from all others. "I called, but no one answered; I spoke, but they did not listen" (Isa. 66:4). God is speaking and demands that we listen; it is crucial that we learn to hear His voice.

Heeding the Voice of God

To hear God's voice, we must begin by abiding in His Word. Many devotional writers of the past employed a method helpful in the beginning steps of this abiding called "praying the Scriptures," a simple yet effective approach.

To begin this exercise, set aside a period in a quiet place, for this form of prayer will take some time to develop. Being silent before the Lord, look to Christ in an attitude of humility, the disposition with which a lamb would approach a shepherd or an infant his mother. It is the conviction of possessing nothing, an attitude of total dependence. Could you gather your own spiritual food? Would you know where to begin to look? Do you have any resources of your own? When you display an attitude of total dependence, the Father will lead you to the true manna that comes from heaven, for He is the true Shepherd who feeds His flock with Himself. He will give you drink from the river of living water, and you will be satisfied. "Truly I say to you, whoever does not receive the kingdom of God like a child shall not enter it at all" (Luke 18:17). As a child, as a lamb, you stand before the Great Provider and surrender your heart, your freedom, your family, and your spiritual needs with joy and confidence, knowing that these could never be managed by one as weak as you. As you do this, you will begin to sense the reality of the great Shepherd, the loving Father, in your spirit. Yes, it will come, not in rushing thoughts or emotions, but in a much deeper and calmer place, the immovable fortress of your spirit. "For we are the true circumcision, who worship in the Spirit of God and glory in Christ Jesus and put no confidence in the flesh" (Phil. 3:3).

The first struggle experienced in this exercise will be with the mind, which will immediately begin to wander. This is only to be expected; your mind has been trained to look outside the body for satisfaction through years of experience. Be encouraged that the mind can be disciplined to look to the Christ within, rather than to work, problems, and past events. After prolonged periods of struggle with your mind, you may give up, believing that God is annoyed with your inability to focus on Him. Nothing could be further from the truth. Attempting to train a wandering mind to concentrate on Him does not displease Him; because of His great love, we are free to fail.

Next, pick a passage from Scripture. I personally recommend Psalm 139. As you approach the Scriptures in this way, you cannot and must not be concerned with the quantity read. One word placed in your heart by God is more valuable than one thousand words memorized. There is a time for academic study, but that time is not now. This will be the only race where the loser, the one who has read the least, will most likely be the winner.

Now open your Bible to Psalm 139 and read the first two words, "O LORD." Do not move past them, silence your mind, turn to Christ within, and listen. Meditate on the words "O Lord." Yes, He is your Lord; all your heart acknowledges it. Praise Him for what that means in your life. "O Lord, You are Lord, and You are responsible to keep me. O Lord, I repent of my worry for tomorrow; I have You, Lord, and You alone are all that I need."

At that, the Scriptures will have accomplished their express purpose, which is not to show you about God, but to actually bring your spirit in touch with God. You no longer need to read about someone who read about someone who read about someone who had heard God, for you have now heard Him yourself. You will be refreshed by just two simple words, "O LORD." Take those words with you throughout the day and greet whatever happens with them.

At this point you are free to move on in the verse to "Thou hast searched me." The very God of the universe taking time to search me! How could I be so important? I possess nothing, and yet I am the focus of His attention.

After you work your way through that psalm, let your next exercise come from Psalm 23. Again begin by silencing your mind and turning your attention to the Christ within. Assured of His presence, you can begin to read the first passage. "The LORD is my shepherd"; let it sink in. Do not merely taste, but swallow! The Lord is *my* Shepherd!

"O praise you, Father, for You, and You alone, are my Provider, my Leader, my Guide, and my Protector. Thank you, Father."

Once this knowledge has moved into your heart, move on. "He makes me lie down in green pastures" (v. 2). Yes, *He makes* you lie down. He leads you to abundance where your soul is filled with the newness of life! Read on. He restores, guides, protects, comforts, and anoints. Yes, " . . . My cup overflows.

Surely goodness and lovingkindness will follow me all the days
of my life, and I will dwell in the house of the LORD forever"
(vv. 5–6). As the knowledge moves from head to heart, the
passage is no longer Scripture written some time past to tell
you about God; it has become the living communication of
God as He reveals Himself to you.

Your time with the Lord will pass very quickly. You will not
want to leave; you will want to take His presence with you,
and this you shall. " . . . And lo, I am with you always, even to
the end of the age" (Matt. 28:20).

Many believe that if they are not able to have a "quiet time"
on a given day, they have missed God, who, they have been
persuaded, can only be met in a special time set aside for Him.
Much damage has been done to our devotional lives by con-
fining God to a time and a place, when Jesus makes it quite
clear that He is within us. Where, then, is this place where we
are to meet Him? The quiet place is within, and this spirit of
ours in which He dwells goes wherever we go. We do not have
to be overly concerned with meeting Him religiously in a particular place each morning, but we are to be consumed with
meeting Him within, moment by moment.

What shall we do when no "quiet time" is available? How
can we worship as we work, drive to our jobs, or do our house-
cleaning? I recommend writing down a small portion of Scripture, to be the message for that week; the piece of paper can
be taken out and read at any time during the day. It will generally take the whole week to finish the passage, but afterward
it will be heart knowledge. Even without any verses written
down, we can recall a familiar passage, the words of a biblical
hymn, or the specifics of how He has worked in our lives. As
we do, we will find ourselves once again realizing that we are
caught up in His presence.

With this type of practice, you will find that it becomes easier and easier to live in unbroken fellowship. You will know the
truth that there is nothing that His presence does not cure.
You will be an effective teacher, for you will possess His teach-

ing. You will even begin to find that when your mind is completely consumed by the projects of the day, your spirit, at the same time, is totally consumed with His presence. I have even found myself praying throughout a conference at the same time I was speaking. This is what the command to pray without ceasing means; it is not unceasing verbal communication, but unbroken communion in the spirit. If you exercise the steps above you will need no one to explain the dynamics of a full life in Christ, for that can become your own experience.

Oh, the privilege of hearing the voice of God, of being one of His sheep who hears His voice, and of having Christ Himself dwelling within; the wonder of no longer being confined to this place or that to worship, but of being able to worship in spirit and in truth anywhere. His voice will always bring a lift in your spirit, even if it comes in the form of conviction, for God only convicts of that from which He fully intends to deliver.

As you hear His voice, it will be important that you heed it. "Therefore, just as the Holy Spirit says, 'Today if you hear His voice, do not harden your hearts'" (Heb. 3:7–8). As you listen, His voice will come in many forms, each for a particular reason. His voice may come as thunder to quiet the questioning mind and demand silence: "Can you thunder with a voice like His?" (Job 40:9). It may pierce like lightning to enlighten and convict: "And He does not restrain the lightnings when His voice is heard" (Job 37:4). He is the mighty Deliverer from all circumstances, so, "The voice of the LORD is powerful" (Ps. 29:4). His voice may be majestic, calling us to worship in silence: "The voice of the LORD is majestic" (Ps. 29:4). His voice can crush all obstacles and assure us: "The voice of the LORD breaks the cedars" (Ps. 29:5). One word from the Lord spoken in your spirit can extinguish all the consuming fires of sin, and He will make a path in the wilderness for you. "The voice of the LORD shakes the wilderness" (Ps. 29:8).

Why did Jesus come? Most answer, "To die for sin." The Book of Hebrews makes it clear that He came to bring us near to God. How many Christians are lacking the experience of God's nearness in unbroken fellowship? Most only stay in the outer court, the soulish life, serving and working for God in their own strength.

Today, resolve not to try to understand or feel the nearness of God. Rather, have faith in the nearness that He has freely given by dwelling in you, and act on the full assurance that He is near. Once you act in faith on the truths God has supplied, you will find that He is indeed as close as the words of your mouth. Let nothing keep you from the enjoyment of His presence!

9

Sharing
in His Victory

I have been asked if Jesus is a racist; my immediate response is *yes*! Without question Jesus is a racist; however, He is not prejudiced against the outer, visible life of man, but against the inner life. The outer life comes in a variety of forms and races, each unique, depending on physical lineage, for the outer life is formed in the womb of the mother. The inner, spiritual life occurs in only two races: either of the lineage of Adam (the life within all of us at birth) or after the life of Christ (which comes at a believer's new birth).

The inner life that is of Adam will take on its own unique shape through perceived identity messages. Satan, in keeping with his stated intent to kill, steal, and destroy, uses events to devise an identity that will consume and ultimately destroy an unsuspecting individual. For example, a child who has lived through his parents' divorce and accompanying feelings of abandonment and insecurity will be tempted to listen to the enemy's voice asserting that the child is unacceptable and worthless. Once this identity is assumed, the child may have to spend the rest of his life trying to undo it.

When we are born again, we receive a new life—Christ's—and a new identity, having lost the old ones at the cross with Jesus (see Gal. 2:20, Rom. 6, and Col. 3). What is true of Christ's life becomes true of the Christian's.

A branch that has been cut off and placed in a vase has no life within it. It may struggle and make every effort to be what it is not—alive—but at last it must accept its miserable condition and give up. A branch grafted into a vine receives new life from the vine, so that what is true of the vine's life will also be true of the branch, which loses its old identity completely and receives a new one.

The condition of the believer who ceases to abide in Christ becomes the same as that of the cut-off branch, even though his position is still in Christ. The baggage of the Adam-life, still resident in the mind, is stirred, resulting in the believer's walking after and expressing the flesh in every aspect of life.

One of the secrets of abiding life is the recognition that Christ is now our life, so what is true about His life becomes true of us, grafted into the vine. He is holy; so are we (1 Peter 2:9-12). He is near to God; so are we. He is acceptable to God, and so are we, since we have received the life that is holy, near, and acceptable. Therefore, as believers we are not to work to gain any of the above; we already have these qualities in Him. We can express the life within, not try to imitate a life above, and we can experience freedom from everything over which Christ gained victory.

From the moment of His death there has existed the possibility for the two types of inner life. Humanity possessed the Adam life, an inner life that had been defeated by temptation, sin, Satan, the world, physical desire, and every kind of circumstance. Christ possessed an inner life that had defeated all the above, even death itself. It is Christ's life, received at our new birth, which gives us victory over every enemy of mankind. This abundant, overcoming life remains a secret to too many believers who work for victory rather than working from the free gift of victory in Him.

Once Christ is your life (He becomes your life when you ask Him to be; it is just that simple), look within and find He is victorious over the sin that has bound you, the identity that has controlled you, and every circumstance that has caused you to turn away. But there is more!

Christ's victory includes triumph over the small and insignificant things of life that become the pebble in your shoe, causing you to stumble or even stop on your new life's journey. What makes man miserable is rarely his inability to obtain or accomplish the grand, but rather his failure in the small and apparently inconsequential. The life of Christ in you has overcome these also! His victory over the apparently small yet experientially gigantic is not one that is observed from afar and then emulated, but a victory in which you already share. As the victory over the insignificant is received, it must be emphasized again and again that you are a partaker—not an imitator—of His life and victory.

The Focus of Freedom

" . . . In the world you have tribulation, but be of good cheer; I have overcome the world" (John 16:33 RSV).

There exists in the Old Testament evidence of a covert, dual complaint. From God it is "Man, you do not know what it is like to be God. I created you for love and fellowship, and yet you desire to live independently." Coming from man, the complaint is "God, You do not understand what it is like to be a man of flesh and bone with desires for both spiritual and carnal life." In love God resolved the conflict by sending the God-Man, fully divine in the spirit but with the soul and body of a man. "And the Word became flesh, and dwelt among us" (John 1:14). It is incredible that this God-Man walked upon the world created through Him among men created in His image, and that He made this statement, a spiritual absolute, that "in the world you shall have tribulation." If the Son of God encountered firsthand the troubles involved in being a man, then we cannot expect to be excluded from similar affliction. However, there is a provision: "in Me you may have peace" (John 16:33). On earth He overcame and therefore freed man from that which had caused him to divide his attentions. No longer must we be pulled between spiritual and carnal. All that is carnal has been overcome *in Him.*

Jesus must become our focus. He alone will give life victory. Man was not created to focus on more than one thing at a time. Being divided causes turmoil, anxiety, depression, worry, and frustration. In Matthew 17:1–9, the writer relates to us that Jesus took Peter, James, and John with Him to the high mountain. When Moses and Elijah appeared, Peter exclaimed, "I will build three tabernacles!"—one for each of the three. Of course this made sense to Peter, who recognized that Moses stood for the law, Elijah represented the prophets, and Jesus was grace and the new covenant. Peter's mistake was equating the three. Immediately a cloud overshadowed them and a voice proclaimed, "This is My beloved Son, with whom I am well pleased; hear Him!" The disciples fell on their faces, Jesus touched them, the cloud departed, and only Jesus remained.

The highest part of a man's being is his heart, made for only one to occupy, that one being Jesus. Once we give anything equal standing with Christ, no matter how good it appears or how great its value in the past, a cloud will immediately overshadow our spirits. We will sense defeat, anger, frustration, and fear. Not until we fall to our faces in submission to the voice proclaiming, "This is My Son," will the cloud (and our spirits) lift.

We should desire in our discipleship and training to remove everything that has equal footing with Christ in the human heart. This one goal for every believer is the issue, not methods. Many suffer from a crowded mountaintop; too many things occupy the place that only Christ is to possess. He is, in fact, King of the mountain.

Imagine a piece of steel five feet long, twelve inches wide, and two inches thick. You are told that you cannot rest until you have driven the object completely into the ground. I suspect that your work would be cut out for you. In fact, I doubt the job could be accomplished in one day, and you would become full of frustration, depression, fear, and anger. However, if a piece of steel were tapered and sharply pointed on the bottom, the task would be much simpler.

Believers lose progress when their lives are not focused on one thing; instead, their lives are blunt with diverse points of interest, activity, and concentration. Marriage, children, sin, others, vocation, and failure all get equal billing with Christ. The average believer is centered on too many things. Only when Christ alone becomes the soul's aim will the believer's life become sharpened and easily able to cut through the daily problems of life. Depression and anger come only when we place something other than Him on the mountain that is the heart. Once we are focused on Him and sharpened, many will try, as with a hammer, to take the edge off our lives, but they will not prevail.

Would you be a happy believer? Then remember there is nothing that the presence of Jesus will not cure. With this in mind, your life can have the focus to drive through any hindrance.

Freedom from the Fear of Being Average

Few believers have found freedom from the fear of being average. Others flee all that is ordinary in pursuit of the great Christian "someday," when problems disappear and opportunity allows for *productivity*, which will allow them to be different, special, blessed, used of the Lord to greatly minister, and made more acceptable than their fellow believers. That great Christian someday will surely allow them to stand out, be counted, and be different. The danger in waiting for this great day is wasting each present moment that could be used to learn that what makes for uncommon believers are the everyday, common events of life.

Jesus was victorious over the fear of being average, and we share in this victory also if His life is our all. He grew up taking care of a widowed mother, with a house full of brothers and sisters, and working at a carpenter's bench day after day. He could have lapsed into feelings of hopelessness and being unfulfilled and too typical, yet His life helped shape and prepare Him for the unique ministry of being so different that men would lift Him up. Does this sound average?

The spiritual man does not make a division between what is secular work and what is spiritual. In Christ the two become one, indistinguishable. For Him the natural (many would call it boring) work of daily life played a part in preparing Him for the supernatural work of God. Why do so many fear that the end result of their run-of-the-mill daily activity will be that they have become merely average people? The answer is that they have separated secular and spiritual work, not allowing the secular to enhance their spiritual life. It is through the events of the average day that spiritual men and women develop.

Once a woman was asked if she did not grow weary from toiling daily over embroidery. "Never!" she exclaimed. "The embroidery is for my wedding dress." The daily, mundane tasks of life become attractive when seen as vital to our preparation for Him. "He who is faithful in a very little thing is faithful also in much; and he who is unrighteous in a very little thing is unrighteous also in much" (Luke 16:10). Do you see that it is in doing the little faithfully that the believer is prepared for true spiritual productivity? You can eliminate labels distinguishing activities of life as small, boring, and insignificant. The making of a sandwich, cleaning the house, paying the bills, running for the children or grandchildren, and the completion of a routine job all work together to enhance our capac-

ity for the holy life, and thus they are as significant as grander
undertakings.

Remember, it is the kingdom of God that is invading this
present world; we are not to allow the world with its ideas of
grandeur to invade the kingdom.

Once we know who we are in Christ, the desire for independent greatness disappears. Without the knowledge of that
in which we share, the sensational and impressive will always
tempt. Jesus was the God-Man possessing all the power of
heaven, and yet He refused to use it to further His cause. He
chose another method to capture the attention of a dying world,
namely conquering and overcoming through serving, humility, and forgiving those who would deny and crucify Him. He
was a relatively quiet man who refused to promote Himself,
and His became the loudest voice in history. Those who promote themselves are soon forgotten; to this day millions promote Him, and He will never be forgotten.

We must share in Christ's liberty from the world of the fan-
tastic and the marvelous. This will be especially important today
when successful self-life is advertised all around us and promoted in the pulpit with the speaker's successes and supernatural activities. Turn on Christian television and the display is
everywhere in the form of self-righteousness, conservative or
liberal correctness, intellectual abilities, personal strength and
boldness, and even fears of such things as the future, the second coming, economic doom, the demise of the schools, or
the upsurge of the occult. These latter topics are promoted by
personalities who advance themselves through the spectacular.

While visiting in South Africa I met with the niece of Andrew Murray, the great devotional writer and evangelist. She
talked to me about several aspects of his life and allowed me
to sit in his chair and read some of his personal letters. The
next day, my brother and I hired a car and traveled quite a distance to visit his grave and the church in which he had minis-
tered and from which had sprung one of the greatest recorded
revivals. It was quite a trip, at no small expense, but that was

of little consequence. I wanted to see the church and his grave, for I admire this man who never exalted himself but celebrated and glorified Christ.

Yet, while traveling in the United States I have often passed by many great monuments built by Christian speakers to testify to their greatness. When asked if I would like to stop, my response is always the same: No! Why? These are but tokens of men exalting themselves. I don't have the time.

Victory over the Family Lineage

Once I was having lunch with an unbelieving friend who made the following statement: "The thing I don't like about you Christians is that you think only those who believe in Jesus Christ as their Savior will go to heaven."

I immediately responded, "That is exactly so!"

He then said that he was able to bring for my examination both a man who was a Christian with wicked behavior and an unbeliever living what he called a holy life. He wanted to know if I would still hold to my confident assertion that only Christians go to heaven.

I then asked him a personal question: "Do you have a son?"

He answered yes.

"How many hours per week does he work?"

"Forty," he replied.

"I have often worked twice that; I work harder than your son!" Next I asked, "How much education does your son have?"

"A bachelor's degree."

"I have more than twice his education. What is his marriage like?"

"He is divorced," he answered.

"I have stayed married to the same woman and work ten times harder than your son at having a good family life!"

At this the man exclaimed, "So what if you are better than my son? What does that prove?"

I replied, "So you agree that I am better than your son?"

"Yes," he said, becoming irritated, "but what's the point?"

"The point is this: Seeing that I have proven myself to be better, I expect you to leave your entire inheritance to me."

"That's ridiculous!" said he. "You may be better, but you are not my son. I will leave you nothing."

I then asked if he had ever heard the term "born again," which I explained was participating in a new birth, receiving a new father, the Father of heaven, and becoming a child of God with full inheritance privileges, not from effort and behavior but through rebirth. The believer who is born of God but has inadequate behavior will not be supplanted by the unbeliever with better conduct. I explained to this friend that he needed a new birth, a new Father, and a new family if he ever hoped to be acceptable to God.

The fact is that as a born-again believer you have a new Father and a new family. You need not be controlled by the old family subculture from which you came. Many believers have come from backgrounds with wickedness in the family trees, drunkenness, adultery, insanity, addictions, explosive tempers, desires to control, molestation, and the list goes on. Often the self-centeredness and fleshly manifestations are passed down from one generation to the next.

I look for my daughter to marry someone like me, for the day she leaves home she'll carry with her an invisible bag containing all the experience and knowledge necessary to manipulate, control, push to a safe limit, and cope with rejection from a guy like me. She will naturally look for someone on whom this behavior is successful, and if he is not like me, she will busy herself making him like me.

So we all come from a family subculture that has helped us adequately or inadequately relate to others. This subculture makes many of us miserable failures at relationships as we repeat family mistakes of the past.

At this point we must remember Christ, who in terms of earthly lineage did not come from a superb family subculture, yet He was victorious over it. In Christ, the born-again believers must share in their new family customs. We are free from the past with its dysfunction and chaos; we are in a new family with its own traditions: love, forgiveness, the freedom for others to offend, peace, patience, kindness, gentleness, and laying down our lives for one another.

Do you believe that you have a new family? Do you believe that the old family no longer binds you and curses you to the fifth generation? It is true! Let no one steal this great secret from you as the new life in God's family begins to encompass you. Have you seen the glory in being cut off and grafted into a new family? Don't wait for others to see it; if necessary be the first to allow the reality of the new family to be expressed through you. Ask the Lord, and He will reveal it to you not only in mind but in heart with heavenly power. With Paul proclaim, "I forget what lies behind," and press on to the free gift of a new family in Christ. In Him your dysfunction has ended. You need not allow the past to continue to control you.

Several of us at a men's retreat witnessed one brother share about the pain he'd suffered after watching his father kill five men. He could think of nothing else but that his father had snuffed out the lives of innocent men, not to mention the happiness of their families. How could he enjoy life when these five men no longer had it? This brother's past family life had become an oppressive point for the enemy. In corporate prayer we all watched as the enemy's stronghold was broken; the brother entered into faith and accepted his place in a new family, freed from the wickedness of the old family subculture. It was glorious!

God is your Father, Jesus is your Brother, and no matter how great the difference between other children of God and yourself, the oneness is greater. Let His victory take hold of your heart!

Freedom from the Rushed Life

Can you find a man in all of history who had more to accomplish than Jesus? He was the Son of God, the Redeemer, the Son of man, the Good Shepherd, and even the Eternal Life. He was to save men from a future hell and the misery of the daily abyss in which men find themselves when living apart from the Father. He was here to establish the kingdom of God within men, which would change the whole of human history! How would He find the time? Would there be enough hours in the day? He would have to make the most of every moment if He were to be *productive*: no time-outs, no cessation of labor, no interval for sickness, no arriving late and leaving early, and no failure to witness. And all of this must be accomplished in the course of His short life. If Jesus did not hurry, all would be lost . . . or would it?

Though there has never been a man with more to do than Jesus, we never find Him in a hurry, in great agitation, or as a nervous wreck. In fact, not only did He spend thirty years in a small village as a carpenter, He also took time out for others and for individual needs (John 11:6). Why was it that God didn't make Jesus rush about more? Could it be that God Himself is not in a hurry? Why did God create the world in seven days, not one? Why does God make His children wait? Why does God invest so much time in each of us, using every circumstance of daily life and even our many failures to create for Himself something unique, beautiful, and useful? Why does the growth of a baby, a forest, or a coral reef take so long? Why? Because hurry, rush, hustle, haste, and speed are not divine attributes. Remember, it was the serpent in the garden that was pressing Eve to act, it was Satan who hurried off to destroy Job, and it was the Pharisees who upon their first encounter with Christ immediately began to plot against Him. Haste is not characteristic of an abiding life but is indicative of the activities of the adversary. The god of hurry is the enemy. Jesus recognized the activity of the enemy in the life of Judas and commanded him to act accordingly by saying, "What you do, do quickly" (John 13:27).

The Christian's life is not hurried but is relaxed and natural. In *active* participation we grow, without worry about memorizing enough Scripture, evangelizing enough people, doing enough church work, and filling every possible minute with activity defined by others as spiritual.

Often I have had believers visiting from what is called the Third World, and after a few days they will ask, "What is your rush?" I have found that these believers are really "First World" when it comes to having a more godly approach to daily living.

While traveling in India, my father and I were treated by some of the brothers to a field trip to observe the last wild herd of Indian elephants. We started very early in the morning with excitement and expectation. However, the day became full of obstacles: a flat tire, a general strike calling for protesters to block all highways, and several miscellaneous delays; in the end we missed the initial boat to take us to the herd. Eventually we did see the elephants, but frankly they were the least enjoyable part of a journey whose hindrances had afforded the opportunity to witness the complete lack of frustration, worry, or hurry in our brothers. In the relaxed Indian manner, each unexpected detainment was met with a simple turning to one another to share our lives, our Lord, and our insights. These believers were not rushed. They were enjoying each moment of the day and our fellowship without the driving need to realize the goal. An inner peace prevailed in these brothers, who lived daily with the kind of delays that on this day were a great blessing to me. We must allow Christ's deliberate lack of speed to grasp and hold us as we find Him in all that surrounds us.

I have found repeatedly that the thing about which I am most anxious is that in which I will undoubtedly fail. While working as an assistant manager in a grocery store, I was given some helpful advice by the manager. "Mike, there is not any decision that needs to be made today, not a single one." I have found that is always true; there is no great hurry today. Also, I have noticed that accelerating the pace of life does not insure more productivity. In a management study it was shown that executives who took an extra thirty minutes for an after-lunch nap were actually 60 percent more productive than those who took no time to rest.

Let the life of Christ set you free from a rushing life that has no time for rest or the enjoyment of family, His creation, and most of all Him!

Victory over the Life of Bitterness

We share in a life that is free from bitterness. Though many failed, abused, and rejected Him, Jesus died with these words, "Father, forgive them; for they do not know what they are doing" (Luke 23:34).

It was brought to my attention that I was being slandered by another brother. My first thought was *this brother should be careful what he says,* for the severest discipline I have personally received from the Lord has come when I have verbally abused His children. The second thought that I had was a prayer, "Father, be as gracious and compassionate to him as you have been to me when I have been in error." Bitterness has no place in the abiding life of Christ, for He met disappointment, defeated it, and overcame bitterness.

Bitterness has its roots in frustration with others. First, many make the mistake of expecting more from the flesh (self-life) than it can give. When my children have had failures, I made it clear that I didn't want to hear them say, "I'll do better"; rather, I wanted to hear them say, "I can't do any better." This awareness can help lead a child out of independence into a deep dependence on the One who dwells within and who has already done better. Second, our frustration with others reveals our lack of spiritual maturity. A believer can become so disappointed with the spiritual progress of his spouse, children, pastor, and church that he rejects them to search for others who he feels will be successful. This is ridiculous in that the next family will not be composed of perfect spiritual giants; the next pastor will have faults; the replacement fellowship will have weaknesses, including someone in the new congregation who will offend.

Sharing in Christ's victory includes seeing those around us through to the end. Jesus could have said, "I'll get some new disciples, because these first ones appear to be in the same condition even after all my efforts." No! He saw them through to the end. Victory is seeing your *present* mate, child, pastor, and fellowship through to the end. To do this your faith must be full of forgiveness, the trait that helps make Christianity what it really is: the expression of God's compassion and love for mankind. When Christianity is void of forgiveness, it becomes difficult, hard, dogmatic, and just another set of teachings that emphasize the correct rules to follow. Forgiveness makes our faith heavenly!

I was once told by a street preacher that the greatest hindrance to people's receptivity to the gospel was the behavior of other believers. This is true; many misrepresent the faith, but none worse than Peter who, after three-and-one-half years of personal instruction by Jesus Himself, cut off a man's ear. Yet Jesus was forgiving and didn't exchange Peter for another more accomplished disciple; victory was taking this man and making him God's man.

Often a mate or a child will misrepresent us, but as we focus on Him we will find freedom from the desire to give up, and thus we can continue with the loved one and allow God to make us His agent of change. We share in this victory, the operative word being *share*. We cannot imitate Jesus' actions, which would only lead to failure and frustration, but we can share in His victory over bitterness, frustration, unforgiveness, and the human weakness of giving up on those around us.

Freedom from the Herd's Standards

When Jesus arrived on the earthly scene, true religious commitment and success were defined by the use of standards already achieved by those who proclaimed them. Jesus brought with him a new definition of success and overcame the worldly measurements. We too share in His victory.

At no point is this victory more important than when it comes to the issue many today have falsely defined: true conversion. This leads the believers who accept the false definition to search for life from Christ rather than to live the life—His life—they already possess.

One particular article in an old devotional book I was reading suggested that there are two ways of entering into Christ: one through an explosion, with fireworks, which was preceded by depression, anxiety, and/or a severe breaking, and the other by coming into Christ slowly, methodically, and through understanding that over a period of time made the journey from head to heart. It was noted that those who come to Christ slowly can rarely tell you the exact day and hour that they gave up on themselves and accepted Christ; however, their lives prove that just such a thing has happened. Of these two methods of coming into Christ, which do you suppose is considered normal and desirable? The explosion, of course! Those who never had the explosion are left wondering if they really do know Christ as well as others. The most interesting point in the article was that in a survey, 60 percent of believers came to Christ the slower way, while 40 percent came by way of the explosion. There is nothing lacking in either, the important fact being that an entrance into Christ did occur. If you have never had the explosion, don't waste time waiting for one; if you have come to Christ slowly, consider yourself in the majority and press on in Him.

The herd would define for us conversion, true godliness, and spirituality. Jesus overcame the false definitions not only of His own generation but of ours as well. Trust His definitions and you may find yourself having a normal Christian experience.

Victory over Grasping

Taking the form of a man, Jesus emptied Himself, which required Him to *receive* daily what was needed from His Father. The carnal teach that we must possess a special endowment or strength in order to receive from God, for it comes through our ability to work hard, to make positive confessions, to follow the proper formula, or in other words, to grasp. Jesus overcame the realm of grasping and opened up for man the concept of receiving.

All that a believer receives must be by faith. It is therefore important to note how a believer accepts the many blessings that God does give through faith.

I liken it to hiking in the mountains and thirstily finding a clear mountain stream. As you cup your hands, the precious water is received, but the tighter you squeeze in an attempt to hold on to the thing you want so much, the less water you will have, until finally there is nothing to drink. The water must be received with no worry of losing it and held gently with confidence.

This is how you are to drink the living water. Don't work to hold on to what God has given, for the moment you become focused on keeping what He freely gives with Himself, you will lose it. You are then focusing on your own effort. All is *given* when He is your focus.

I remember early on doing an Abiding Life Seminar; I kept working to abide in Christ, knowing that I wanted others to receive from the Lord, not from me. By the middle of the week I was exhausted! I realized that I *was* abiding, not because of effort, but because Christ placed me in Himself in an abiding relationship. I stopped working, put my eyes on

Him, thanked Him for abiding, rested, and experienced life in Him the rest of the week. I simply received abiding, no longer grasping for it.

Share in His relaxed life by receiving!

Overcoming the World of Pain

Did Christ experience pain? The answer is yes. In Him, though, pain was not senseless but had a purpose. When we are in Him our pain becomes a wonderful expectation.

Often I'm asked the question "Are Christians supposed to suffer, to experience difficult times, and generally to find themselves unhappy?" Pain and suffering are common to all of humankind. Outwardly, the believer suffers like the unbeliever, from nature, others, or the physical body, but Christians need not experience the destructive inward suffering that plagues those who do not know the Lord. I often note in our discipleship sessions that Christians have had similar calamities and yet have not all responded in a like manner—some with depression, anger, frustration, or none of the above. Life seems to deal its blows without partiality, and yet the response is varied; the same event occurring in two believers' lives often elicits two different reactions. Why? It all depends on the inner attitude of the one suffering. It has been said that what becomes of us in the long run depends on what life finds in us. Suffering makes some bitter and others sweet. What matters is not what happens to us, but what we do with the event afterward.

In the mountains it is not uncommon at all to see a half-dead aspen tree. The sun shines on all but brings increased life to one branch and quickened decay to the other, depending on what is inside the branch. As with the sun, suffering leaves some withered and weak and others, because of the life within, stronger and more prepared for any amount of suffering.

I remember discipling two women, each one suffering at the hand of an unfaithful husband who sought to justify his behavior by picking his wife apart. One woman became absolutely radiant through her suffering, for she found Christ to be her all; the other became bitter and, to be honest, quite ugly, as her inward stress disfigured her. Two women, same event, and different responses. One possessed an inner life that had met rejection and had overcome with love; the other had been overcome by the rejection.

As a believer I cannot always determine what happens to me, but I can determine how it will affect me. If I am driven closer to the Lord, then the event will make me happy, more useful, and full of life. The common events of life can either make me common or spiritually alive.

Never deal with pain on a human level; bring God into your pain and allow Him to guide you through it. You will find that God takes what appears to be senseless suffering and turns it into spiritual life. The suffering may even have its roots in evil; but the issue is still not whence calamity comes but rather where you allow it to take you. Place God in the center of your pain, and He will guide you to deeper life. The cross is the perfect example of God-guided pain, for this great suffering became life not only to Christ but to millions.

There is one more important reason for pain, which is to bring us to the end of trusting ourselves, the source of much misery. Many call this brokenness. It is not a prerequisite for the achievement of this state that a person must be a drug addict, clinically depressed, or a gutter resident. It can arrive very quietly in the deepest recesses of a man's heart with none of those manifestations. It is simply giving up on our independence from God.

Recently, while staying in a mountain cabin, I noticed a moth beating its wings against the window in a vain attempt to escape. I decided that I would attempt its capture and release, but the more I tried to help the moth the harder it tried to escape. Not until it became totally exhausted and unavoidably relaxed was I able to pick it up and free it. Many believers are wound so tightly they are beating their inner-man's wings against the invisible forces of life that bind and enslave them; the only possible solution they know is to *try harder*. They must let God be God without attempting to usurp His responsibilities in order to become relaxed souls whom the Father takes into His hands and thus gives freedom.

Yes, believers suffer, and we must thank God for being in the midst of all the unpleasantness by which He perfects those whom He loves.

Victory over the Insignificant

I have a file that is labeled "So What?"; into it I place everything that is inconsequential, irrelevant, slight, petty, and immaterial. I want to share in His victory over these things. I want to be as free from the insignificant as He was. "For you tithe mint and dill and cummin, and have neglected the weightier provisions of the law. . . . You blind guides, who strain out a gnat and swallow a camel!" (Matt. 23:23–24).

There was a man who survived an airplane crash in which many died. His reaction was to wander around among the bodies looking for his briefcase! Many believers behave similarly when they wander through a dying world searching for the insignificant. Has there ever been a time when the church needed to share in this victory over the insignificant more than today? The Christian family is pressured by a culture that is pitted against the parent, by godless, glamorized life-styles and by temptations that abound for every member of the family. Yet these things are rarely considered! Instead, in the midst of the family carnage we look for the briefcase containing the desire for our mates to confess the misplaced word that caused offense, the anger due to others who don't agree with us, the upset state that occurs if others aren't sympathetic toward our hurts, the fights over who said what and who did what, and the accusations against those who do not notice our efforts.

"Lord! Please deliver your people not only from what is bad and evil but also from what is not worthy of their attention. Let us see that not only did the Son overcome sin, but He also overcame the insignificant."

Does your family or fellowship, those with whom you labor, traffic in the unimportant? If so, ask yourself how the discussions concerning such things as the color of the church carpet, which way the toilet paper rolls off the holder, where your clothes are left, what kind of shoes your children buy, and how much gasoline was left in the auto fit into the world as Christ saw it. If they don't fit, then flee the petty, for the longer we traffic in it, the more like it we become.

Victory over Isolation

Following Christ has put you in the minority; few will agree with—let alone encourage you in—your endeavors. But take heart; Jesus was victorious over the fear of isolation that comes from being in the minority. Those who were counted with the multitudes present on the day that Christ was crucified were actually the farthest from Him. Being in the majority will always distance you from the Savior. Counting yourself with the minority will place you nearest to Christ. His life (which is our life, Col. 3:4) stood fast in being different from the majority; He did not isolate Himself under pressure from others over His nonconforming views.

Church history is cluttered with so-called spiritual hermits who withdrew from the world, believing this would allow them unhindered access to God. In Jesus, however, we see a man who had perfect passage to God and yet remained in the midst of humanity and its most significant issues. He confronted the burdens of the world around Him; "He set His face toward

Jerusalem." Knowing that He held the minority view never caused Him to withdraw.

Today many are running from the crises that exist in their own cultures; they fear being in the minority, so they emphasize separation from the world, survival fellowships in the desert, and hiding in communities of believers. It is true that in many ways they are free from the burdens of our society, but merely because they refuse to take on any of the burdens, which in Him are quite easy to carry.

A professional psychologist once stated, "You are never to take the counselees' problems home with you."

My response was, "The day I don't take their problems home with me is the day I will no longer counsel." If my daughter were to tell me her marriage was falling apart, would I give her one hour of my time and then state, "That's all the time I have! I cannot think of your problems any longer"? Of course not! I would carry that burden in the Lord until the problem was resolved. And if a brother or sister in Christ were to send a daughter to me who stated the same trouble with her marriage, I would also carry that burden with me until the problem was resolved.

The Christ in whom we abide bore the burdens of the whole world! As we share in His life, we can carry the problems of those around us without being crushed. We need not withdraw from the world because of the fear of others' difficulties or of being in the minority. He stood fast; we share in His life, so now we stand fast.

I must ask if you are content to be in the minority, not only in the world, but also many times in the Christian community. If you abide in His life, His heavenly, unique principles will flow through you, and you *will* be different. The majority emphasize big accomplishments; the minority must prove its faithfulness in the small. The majority promise an immediate fix for all problems by simply following a formula; the minority teach a moment-by-moment freedom that comes from our fellowship with Christ. The majority will continue to emphasize what they have that others do not; the minority see what others cannot—the fullness of Christ in every believer—and work to reveal this treasure to all who already possess it. The majority point to the greatness of their faith as evidenced by immediate results; the minority say faith increases in direct proportion to how long one waits without receiving. The majority accentuate knowledge, a full notebook, and a heavy heart carrying burdens that only Christ is able to carry; the minority display a full heart weighted down with love. The majority are hard and stand on the Law, telling of God's judgment and making believers competitive or hopeless; the minority reveal the grace and compassion of a loving God who will take us on in spite of failure as we simply turn to Him with repentant hearts. The majority stress knowing the Book, the minority the Author. The majority list the daily steps needed to secure the presence of God, while the minority tell of God's activities securing us daily. The majority have a favored word, *change*; the minority say by faith we must *expand* what we already have in Christ.

The majority would fit the believer with glasses that allow him to see only what must be done and leave him working *for* holiness; the minority want all to see what Christ has done for them, to be encouraged that they can work *from* His holiness (1 Peter 2:9–12). The majority do not allow for the enjoyment a new believer has in his walk and immediately lay on burdens. The majority never separate what is of the soul (knowledge, ability, talent, and appearance) from what is of the spirit. The minority find strength in the Spirit and put no confidence in the flesh. The majority teach that we must generate faith and grasp hold of truth; the minority know that the things of faith are received. The majority say, "Strive to be like Christ"; the minority acknowledge that we are one in spirit with Him. The majority stand before God with confidence in their performance, knowing that they have earned a hearing; the minority kneel before God expecting to be heard because the Son has won the audience. The majority point out the weakest of men as proof that we need a Savior; the minority notice the failures of the most talented and knowledgeable as proof of the need of a Savior. The majority are fatalistic, seeing no joy until heaven in the future; the minority have found true life today and are full of hope. The majority say, "Do right," but the minority encourage that we choose right. The majority focus on our sins, as the minority promote the answer to our sins. The majority say we must agree on every doctrine; the minority maintain we must agree in the attitude of love. The majority follow a teaching, while the minority follow the Teacher. The majority are easily offended, believing they are justified in their attitude; the minority live by the spiritual absolute that no matter what the offense, we are commanded to love without excuse.

If you abide in Christ and share in His life, you live in the minority. Are you pleased to be there? There is no better place! Here you will take a stand in the midst of many obstacles, trials, and issues, such as a difficult marriage, a rebellious child, an unsatisfying job, and much resistance. You must stand, for if you withdraw from these, you will find yourself withdrawing from the One who would see you through them and being drawn to the old idols of the past to try to conquer the problems. Jesus, in the minority, stood fast; we share in this life, also.

Victorious over the Enemy

"I was watching Satan fall from heaven like lightning. Behold, I have given you authority to tread upon serpents and scorpions, and over all the power of the enemy, and nothing shall injure you" (Luke 10:18–19). We fight a defeated foe. This must not be forgotten. We fight from, not for, a position of victory. We share in a life that has overcome the enemy! Though Satan is vicious, he is defeated.

Once after a long day of discipling those who had been blinded by the enemy, I was especially drawn to prayer, for I could easily see the schemes of the enemy in the pits he was digging for the unsuspecting. I was so focused on the enemy's power, deception, and ability to confuse, thwart, and destroy that all I could see was the pit, the pit, the enemy and his pit! The next week I observed something wonderful: The pit the enemy had dug made a believer so miserable that he turned to God with renewed desire to stay in constant, moment-by-moment fellowship with the Son. With the dirt thrown out of the pit Satan created, a mound was built that led to the very presence of God. The enemy could never be persuaded to build a hill to God, but he will actively dig a pit that indirectly results in such an elevated heap. It has been my experience over and over again that God does make the pit a mountain of success. Therefore, let every obstacle, defeat, adverse circumstance, and experience of both 1 Corinthians 4 and 2 Corinthians 4 be the mounds that drive you into the very presence of God. Never fear the pit; with eager expectation, let Christ take you up the mound!

Life That Is Simple

We want Christ's life and His victory in which we share to become more than just a teaching; we want it to become our way of life. But how? Simply by being in Him. In the world we have tribulation; in Him we have peace. But how, again you ask? By accepting the fact that we are in Him, not by self-effort but because He placed us there the day we were born again. You share in His life, so you can say, "Christ is my life." This statement affirms what is true. I have often been accused of teaching a method that is too simple to believe; that, of course, is the hindrance of a message of simple faith. Myriad believers still find it difficult, if not impossible, to act on.

The deepest life in Christ is most suited for the very weak, a category into which we all fall, though few admit it. Man needs the Creator to maintain his fragile existence. Those who acknowledge dependence will readily say, "I cannot overcome.

There is no way for me to do it. I have tried all, vowed all, and I cannot; I can now only state that Christ is my life." Once this statement is made, the fact will be experienced; His life will flow in every turmoil, in everything unexpected, in every battle, and in every relationship. Why? Because He says He is our life! He is with us, in us; He is the Vine and we are the branches; it is so because He says it is so. This is faith! This is enough! We do not require experiential or emotional proof, but only His telling us so. This is the abiding life!

For information on conferences or a study guide, please write:

Abiding Life Ministries International
P.O. Box 620998
Littleton, CO 80162